THUNDERING THROUGH THE CLEAR AIR

No.61 (Lincoln Imp) Squadron at War

Best Wishes
Derek Brammer

By
Derek Brammer

First printed in 1997
Second Edition published in Great Britain in 2005
by **TUCANN***books*

ISBN 1 873257 57 0

Published by TUCANN*books*,
19 High Street, Heighington, Lincoln LN4 1RG
Tel & Fax: 01522 790009 • www.tucann.co.uk

PREFACE

During the Second World War I grew up in the Cathedral City of Lincoln. By the end of 1943 the Royal Air Force had thirteen Bomber Command airfields within a twelve mile radius of its ancient city walls.

The closest airfield to my home was only two miles away at RAF Skellingthorpe. Like many of my schoolboy friends during this period it was the daily sights and sounds of aircraft from this airfield that fired my imagination and began a lifelong interest in air warfare.

Even now I vividly remember the tremendous tumult of sound generated by the aircraft of No.50 and No.61 Squadrons as they took-off for a bombing operation. Later, in the early hours of the morning I would be awakened by the sound of returning aircraft racing across the early morning sky to be the first home.

In 1994 I was given a photograph of a Lancaster with 118 bomb symbols painted on the fuselage below the cockpit window. My curiosity was aroused and research revealed the aircraft was Lancaster ED860 QR-N "Nan" of No.61 Squadron which had been based at Skellingthorpe in 1943-44. Further investigation revealed that ED860 went on to complete 130 operations over enemy territory before it crashed on take-off in October 1944.

My research into the operational record of ED860 produced many more fascinating facts and interesting stories from the men who flew operations with No.61 Squadron, Bomber Command. This is their story.

Derek Brammer

Contents

Photographs

Introduction

This book is not intended to appraise the ethics or the offensive strategy of the Royal Air Force bombing campaign against Germany between 1939-1945. It is the story of No.61 Squadron Bomber Command at war, and a tribute to the brave young men who volunteered to fly dangerous bombing operations against enemy targets on mainland Europe.

After the fall of France in 1940 the only war front accessible to an isolated Britain was the air front i.e. the skies over Nazi Germany and occupied territory.

The offensive arm of the Royal Air Force, Bomber Command, had only been formed in 1936 and unfortunately its front line bomber squadrons were numerically weak and ill-prepared to carry out the enormous task they were givenby the War Cabinet. This situation resulted in appalling operational losses in the first two years of the war and by the end of 1941 Bomber Command's future was in doubt.

In February 1942 Air Marshal Arthur Travers Harris was appointed Air Officer Commanding-in-Chief of Bomber Command to carry out the Air Ministry's new policy of "Area Bombing" against the major industrial cities of Germany.

After the introduction of the Avro Lancaster, new navigation equipment and improved operational tactics the Command's aircrew morale gradually improved, but the casualty figures did not. During the period 1942-44 operational aircrew only had a one in three chance of surviving a tour of 30 sorties over enemy held territory. In spite of these discouraging odds the young men of Britain and the Commonwealth continued to volunteer for aircrew duty with the squadrons of Bomber Command.

As one of the original members of No.5 Group (Bomber) the aircraft of No.61 Squadron flew more raids than any other Lancaster squadron between 1942-45 and the second highest number of bombing raids overall in Bomber Command during the Second World War.

By the spring of 1945 Bomber Command had almost closed the huge gap that had existed in 1939 between strategic desirability and operational capacity in both strength and technical ability. However, the price paid in aircrew lives continued to be high right to the end of the conflict.

CHAPTER 1

BOMBER COMMAND 1939-1945

The Royal Air Force bombing campaign against Germany started on the very first day of the war, 3rd September 1939, and finished five and a half years later on the 2nd-3rd May 1945 with an attack on the German port of Kiel. It was the first time in warfare that such a sustained aerial bombardment by aircraft had been used as a strategic offensive weapon against an enemy.

During this period the squadrons of RAF Bomber Command flew 389,808 sorties over enemy territory for the loss of 8,953 aircraft. They also suffered a total of 55,563 aircrew fatalities. The dangers faced by RAF aircrew during the Second World War were many but the two that took the greatest toll of life were hostile enemy action and flying accidents during training.

Bomber Command's operational strength after the fall of France in 1940 was only 23 front line squadrons containing a total of about 350 aircraft with trained crews. However most of these crews, apart from the Whitley squadrons of No.4 Group, had little or no night flying experience and navigation aids were virtually non-existent. Squadrons were equipped with twin-engine Wellington, Whitley, and Hampden, the so called heavy bombers of the day, and the medium range day bomber Blenheim. All suffered from poor defensive speed and armament against fast German single-engine day fighters.

By late 1940 the Air Staff reluctantly admitted that the 1930s theory of self-defending daylight bomber formations had been found wanting when faced with determined fighter opposition. It was decided to discontinue further large daylight bombing raids over enemy held territory as it would impose unacceptable losses to both aircrew and machines. Bomber Command had no alternative but to become essentially a night raiding force. However, the difficulty of finding and bombing distant targets at night in all kinds of weather without navigation and blind bombing aids still remained. It was not uncommon during the first two years of the war for even experienced RAF aircrew to become lost in daylight while flying cross-country training flights in the U.K.

The Butt Report:

In the spring of 1941 an investigation was instigated by Professor Lindemann, Churchill's scientific advisor, to show the deficiencies of Bomber Command as a night bombing force and the plight of the young bomber crews. The investigation was headed by Mr D.M.Butt, a civil servant in the War Cabinet Secretariat. The resulting confidential Butt Report analyzed Bomber Command's operational performance during June and July 1941 by studying hundreds of target aiming point and daylight reconnaissance photographs. It highlighted the difficulties faced by a bomber force that was equipped with daylight bombers trying to find distant targets at night over hostile enemy territory, using only basic methods of navigation.

The report showed that only one in three of the attacking aircraft on distant German targets were bombing within five miles of the target aiming point during a full moon period. While in the moonless period of the month, only one in twenty of the bomber crews got within the five mile zone. The situation was even worse when you consider that only the crews who reported bombing the target were used for the analysis. At least 33% of the crews dispatched during this period didn't even claim to have bombed the primary targets.

Navigation and Weather:

The standard method of navigation required a course to be worked out from base to the first turning point using the forecast wind speed and direction. It was important to identify a landmark en route to check the wind speed at the height flown before computing the next leg of the flight.

Weather was always a big factor in night flying operations, and if cloud obscured all below then navigators used Dead Reckoning (DR) until a visual astro or radio transmission fix could be ascertained. By this time, due to the wind factor, the aircraft could be miles off the planned course.

The problem of forecasting weather was difficult even in the United Kingdom where the organisation necessary to obtain and collate data was readily available, but to forecast weather conditions over distant enemy territory was much more difficult. Nevertheless, detailed and accurate information regarding the weather to be expected en route or over the target area was an integral part of Bomber Command's operational planning.

It can therefore be said that the information gathered by the Meteorological Flight proved itself to be an indispensable part of Bomber Commands operations over Germany.

New Policy and New Chief for Bomber Command:
Bomber Command's overall performance during 1940-41 proved that it was impossible for front line squadrons to carry out precision bombing raids at night. After suffering heavy aircraft losses during the fourth quarter of 1941, the roll of Bomber Command and the strategic bombing campaign was debated at the highest level. As a result, the Air Ministry issued a new directive for future bombing operations against Germany on 14th February 1942.

The Command was ordered to focus its operations on dislocating the German transportation system and to try and destroy the morale of the enemy civilian population, particularly that of the industrial worker engaged in the production of war materials. Also the Command would, on occasion, be called upon to make diversionary attacks on German naval units and submarine-building yards.

The policy was not entirely new as the Air Ministry had, since October 1940, been encouraging Bomber Command to devote some of its effort to area bombing attacks on German cities. Eight days after the new directive was issued, Air Marshal Arthur Harris was appointed AOC in C Bomber Command.

Although Harris (now Sir Arthur) did not formulate the new policy he did over the next three years enthusiastically carry out the directive of an area bombing campaign against many of the large German industrial cities.

Harris was dedicated to the belief that the war could be brought to a close quickly through a massive onslaught by heavy bomber squadrons on German cities. He wanted the Americans to join Bomber Command in an all out effort to wipe out Berlin in the winter of 1943-44. Unfortunately for Harris, the American air force commanders favoured high altitude daylight precision bombing operations against oil fields, aircraft factories and associated industrial targets. However, the 8th Air Force bombardment groups soon faced the same problem Bomber Command had faced three years before, i.e. how to protect slow heavy bomber aircraft on deep penetration daylight missions from being attacked and destroyed by fast single-engine German fighters. It would be another eighteen months before the American fighter groups had a long range fighter capable of escorting their heavy bombers all the way to Berlin. In the meantime, the American bomber groups suffered ever increasing losses the deeper they penetrated German airspace.

Development of Navigational Aids and Blind Bombing Systems : German scientists had developed an aircraft blind landing system called Lorenz for civil aviation use in the mid-thirties. Basically, it was a short range radio system which used two-directional beam aerials and radiated two wide beams of radio signals which overlapped the centre of the runway. These aerials were alternatively switched to transmit, so that one radiated only morse dots along the final approach path and the other only dashes. Also the spacing of the dots and dashes was such that where the beams overlapped a continuous note was received, indicating to the pilot that he was flying in line with the centre of the runway. Later, the RAF adopted a similar system called the Standard Beam Approach (SBA). This system radiated Morse A to the left and Morse N to the right of the continuous centre line beam note.

By the start of the war, the German scientists had secretly developed the Lorenz system into a long range, ultra short wave blind bombing system called Knickerbein. This radio triangulation system used two powerful transmitters situated 200 miles apart which beamed narrow radio signals at British cities. In essence, during a raid, all a Luftwaffe bomber pilot had to do was fly his aircraft along the approach beam until the second radio beam was detected over the target, then the observer dropped the bombs.

British scientific intelligence managed to identify the existence of Knickerbein in 1940 through the inspection of crashed Luftwaffe aircraft and the interrogation of aircrew. Once the radio frequencies used by the system had been established, counter measures were quickly taken against its effectiveness.

However, within a few weeks the Germans introduced Knickerbein's sophisticated successor, X-Gerat. This equipment was fitted in the Luftwaffe Pathfinder aircraft and used with great success during the winter bombing campaign against English cities in 1940-41.

Meanwhile the development of the long overdue British navigational aid called Gee was approaching completion by the Telecommunications Research Establishment. Trials of the Gee (for grid) system, took place over the U.K. during the spring and summer of 1941 followed by operational flights over Germany in August of the same year.

The Gee box in the aircraft measured the difference in time taken to receive pulse signals from three widely separated ground stations in England. The signal received was displayed upon a cathode ray tube on the navigators table; with a special Gee grid overprinted on his map, it gave him the aircraft's position to within 5 miles at best. Even this accuracy depended on a number of factors, as did the effective range which varied between 300-400 miles depending upon the height of the receiving aircraft.

After two years of blindly groping their way at night and in adverse weather conditions the RAF bomber crews at last had airborne navigation equipment to help them find targets such as Germany's industrial Ruhr valley.

By the start of 1943 two blind bombing aids called H2S and Oboe were being installed in Bomber Command aircraft.

H2S was the first airborne radar set which showed an image of the prominent ground features below the aircraft on the screen of a cathode ray tube. It was an exciting development for the bomber crews and seemed to fulfil all the requirements to help the navigators identify cloud covered targets from high altitude. Initially only the aircraft of No.8 Group Pathfinder squadrons had the H2S sets installed to aid them in marking a target more accurately. However, the equipment suffered a lot of teething troubles and was found to perform best over rivers or estuaries where a clear distinction could be made between the water and land mass.

The second device called Oboe was a more sophisticated variation of the German X-Gerat system. During trials carried out over Lorient and St. Nazaire in December 1942 the device proved accurate to a remarkable 600 yards on tests. Unfortunately the Oboe system suffered from two limiting factors. First, Bomber Command possessed only two sets of ground stations at the outset, and therefore could only control twelve Pathfinder aircraft an hour over the target area. Second, the Oboe radio beams, like the Gee navigation system, had a limited range from the English ground stations due to the curvature of the earth. Both could cover the Ruhr but not much further if a heavy bomber was flying below 20,000 feet. In order to get the best range possible out of the Oboe equipment it was installed in the high flying Pathfinder Mk.IX Mosquitoes which had an operational height of 30,000 feet.

The following year two pieces of defensive electronic equipment were installed in the heavy bomber aircraft. The Monica and Fishpond units detected aircraft that were close by in the bomber stream, while Boozer gave early warning to bomber crews of German predicted flak and searchlight radar.

During the five year bombing campaign both sides took radio counter measures against air to ground communications, blind bombing and navigation aids. So it was not surprising that within a few months of the British electronic aids being introduced, the German scientists had developed equipment that could jam Gee ground transmissions from England and airborne radar apparatus that enabled their night fighters to pick up the transmissions from H2S from a distance of over 100 miles. While the pulses picked up from the Monica equipment resulted in the loss of many unsuspecting crews of Bomber Command.

Pathfinders:

The most significant bombing raid innovation adopted by Bomber Command during the whole of the Second World War was the formation in 1942 of No.8 Group specialist Pathfinder squadrons. Their sole purpose was to fly in advance of the main bombing force to identify and mark the target. They carried specially designed route marker flares and coloured Target Indicators (TIs) that were bright enough to be seen from a great height amidst the smoke of a burning city.

The most frequently used technique was for an advance party of Pathfinders, known as the Illuminators, to find the target area and light it up with a line of white flares. They were quickly followed by a group called the Visual Markers who identified the actual target aiming point and marked it with coloured flares. Following close behind came the third group called the Backers Up who dropped incendiaries on the coloured flares. Then came the main bombing force, which dropped incendiaries and high explosive 4000 lb Cookies which caused blast damage and spread the incendiaries.

Over the following months many refinements were added to the Pathfinder marking techniques plus new pyrotechnics like the hooded flare which was fitted with a barometric fuse to ensure it exploded at the right height, thus reducing dazzle to the following main force. Sky marking a cloud covered target was given the code word Wanganui and brilliantly coloured red and yellow flares would be used. For ground marking a target with red and green TIs the code word was Newhaven or Parramatta when H2S was used.

The Mk.XIV stabilised bombsight was also introduced in 1942 and was first issued to the Pathfinder squadrons. Its biggest advantage over the old course setting Bombsight was that it did not demand the same rigid approach up to the target.

Bomber Stream:

This system was also devised in 1942 to control large numbers of aircraft over a target while at the same time overwhelming the enemies defences. It was first used on 30th-31st May 1942 when 1,047 aircraft were dispatched on a night bombing raid against Cologne. In essence, all the aircraft were briefed to fly a common route and speed to the target divided only by each aircraft's individual height and time slot, both en-route and over the target. The recent introduction of the Gee navigation equipment made it easier for the bomber crews to navigate within precise safety limits in the stream to minimise the risk of collision.

Aircraft:

During 1941 the bomber squadrons received two new four-engine bomber types called Stirling and Halifax. The Short Brothers Stirling began operations with daylight attacks in February 1941. Though it looked extremely impressive with vast length and unprecedented height it soon became unpopular with aircrew because of its poor operational ceiling and sluggish manoeuvrability except at low level. Although it could lift a heavy bomb load it could not carry bombs larger than a 2000 lb high explosive (HE). By mid 1943 it had been withdrawn from front line squadrons because of appalling operational losses and used as a glider tug or general transport.

The Handley Page Halifax was originally designed to the P13/36 specification with a gross weight of 26,300 lb powered by two Vulture engines and first flew in 1937. By this time the need for larger heavy bombers was envisaged so the Halifax was developed further into a four-engine heavy bomber first using Rolls Royce Merlin X engines and later fitted with Bristol Hercules engines. Though it never attained the limelight of the Lancaster, the Halibag made a tremendous contribution to the RAF bombing campaign.

About the same time A.V. Roe designed the twin-engine Manchester and this aircraft was introduced during November 1940 to replaced the ageing Hampden aircraft of 5 Group. Unfortunately the new Rolls Royce Vulture engines used on the Manchester were not a success and resulted in the loss of many aircraft and experienced aircrew. In spite of its un-reliable engines the basic Manchester airframe design was considered very good and a decision was taken in 1940 to build a longer wing-span version using four Rolls Royce Merlin XX engines.

These changes brought about the evolution of a new heavy bomber called the Lancaster which was capable of delivering a 11,000 lb bomb load to German targets and, with modifications, a 22,000 lb Grand Slam bomb over a shorter range.

Deliveries of the Lancaster to the Bomber squadrons started in December 1941 and it proved to be the best British aircraft of its type during the war.

The basic aircraft however was still a day-bomber designed to a self-defending specification issued by the Air Ministry in 1936, and as a result the Lancaster squadrons were to suffer high aircrew casualties over the next three years. Apart from the inherent dangers of flying in a bomber stream at night and the lack of friendly night fighter cover, the aircraft's low calibre machine guns were incapable of deterring rear and beam attacks from enemy fighters. It was also defenceless against the German night fighters fitted with two upward firing 20 mm cannon.

Nonetheless, by the end of the war in May 1945, approximately 6,500 of the 7,366 Lancasters built had flown 156,192 operational sorties and dropped over 600,000 tons of bombs on German and Italian targets. Unfortunately the cost was high. Between February 1942 and May 1945, 3,431 Lancasters and approximately 24,000 aircrew failed to return from operations.

Aircrew:
The personal qualities required of the young men selected for aircrew duties was never compromised during the whole campaign.

In 1936 the Secretary of State for Air announced that the number of recruits into the RAF Voluntary Reserve would increase from 60 to 800 per year. Originally the Reserve was only for civilians who wanted to become pilots but because of the RAF expansion programme other technical trades started to be trained as well.

Many years of interviewing experience was needed to enable RAF trade selection officers choose potential air crew.

The criteria for choosing a candidate for Elementary Flying Training was not purely a matter of intelligence and physical fitness. What interviewing officers considered to be the most important ingredient was the temperament of the individual and would he cope with the pressures of air warfare.

RAF training was extremely thorough and designed to breed self confidence into a young pilots ability, the aircraft he flew and eventually his crew. It was the RAF's thorough training that provided crew discipline and spirit.

Even in the face of heavy losses morale was sustained by the knowledge that each individual believed he was part of the best aircrew in Bomber Command and therefore would survive his 30 sortie operational tour.

Approximately 62% of the 125,000 men who served as aircrew in Bomber Command during the war became casualties. Of these, 52% were sustained while flying operations and a further 10% while on non-operational flights within the U.K.

CHAPTER 2

No.61 SQUADRON 1917-1919

No.61 Squadron was first formed at Rochford airfield, Essex, on 2nd August 1917 as part of the Royal Flying Corps London Air Defence Force.

The Squadron, commanded by Major Prettyman, became the first of three home based fighter squadrons to be equipped with the nimble Sopwith Pup in order to combat the threat of German daylight bombing raids on London.

The Squadron, led by a Western Front veteran called Captain Cecil Lewis, went into action for the first time 10 days later, when sixteen Pups attacked a formation of ten German Gothas bombers flying over the Thames Estuary. The enemy formation was turned back over Rochford airfield where they dropped two bombs before getting away.

Although the Pups chased the Gothas 40 miles out to sea, they were unable to claim any decisive victories over the attacking force. This was the Squadron's only taste of action in World War 1.

In December 1917 No.61 Squadron was to provide the nucleus of pilots for the formation of No.141 Squadron and started to re-equip with S.E.5a fighters. The change over was never completed as the aircraft was found to be unsuitable for night fighting.

At about midnight on 7th March 1918 a tragedy occurred when the Squadron suffered its first operational loss. Captain Henry Clifford Stroud was returning to base after a night flying patrol when his aircraft was involved in a mid-air collision with an aircraft belonging to No.37 Squadron. Both pilots fell to their deaths just outside the village of Rayleigh and were buried in the RFC/RAF plots at Rochford parish churchyard.

Unofficial memorials were erected to both these young military flyers at the place where the bodies were found. At the end of 1918 the Squadron began to receive Sopwith Camels and continued on home defence duties at Rochford until it was disbanded on 1st June 1919.

Anson Aircraft of the reformed No.61 Squadron at RAF Hemswell 1937

No.61 Squadron Hampdens flying over Lincolnshire in 1940

Manchester L7521 QR-W from RAF Woofox Lodge in 1941

Manchester L7521 crashed attempting to land at RAF Waddington in 1942

Lancaster Mk.II DS604 was lost over Frankfurt 11th April 1943

Lancaster Mk.III PB759 QR-N lost Pölitov raid 8th February 1945

CHAPTER 3

No.61 SQUADON 1937-1945

The Squadron was reformed at RAF Hemswell near Lincoln on 8th March 1937 as part of the mid-thirties panic expansion of the Royal Air Force.

Squadron Motto:	**Per Purum Tonantes** (Thundering Through The Clear Air)
Badge:	**The Lincoln Imp.** (Associates the Squadron with the district in which it was reformed in 1937.)
Service:	**No.5 Group Bomber Command** from the outbreak until the end of World War Two, with short detachments to Coastal Command in November/December 1940 and July/August 1942.

Squadron Aircraft Codes:		
	61	March 1937-March 1939
	LS	March 1939-September 1939
	QR	September 1939-April 1951

No. 61 SQUADRON COMMANDING OFFICERS 1937-1945

COMMANDING OFFICERS	Date
Squadron Leader C H Brill	March 1937
Wing Commander C M De Crespigny	September 1939
Wing Commander F M Denny	February 1940
Wing Commander G H Sheen	May 1940
Wing Commander G E Valentine	November 1940
Wing Commander C T Weir	September 1941
Wing Commander C M Coad	June 1942
Wing Commander W M Penman	February 1943
Wing Commander R N Stidolph	October 1943
Wing Commander J B Tait	April 1944
Wing Commander A W Doubleday	July 1944
Wing Commander R D Pexton	September 1944
Wing Commander C W Scott	February 1945

RAF Airfields:

HEMSWELL:	March 1937 - July 1941
NORTH LUFFENHAM:	July 1941 - October 1941
WOOLFOX LODGE:	October 1941 - May 1942
SYERSTON:	May 1942 - November 1943
SKELLINGTHORPE:	November 1943-February 1944
CONINGSBY:	February 1944 - April 1944
SKELLINGTHORPE:	April 1944 - June 1945

Aircraft Type:

AUDAX & ANSON	1937 - 1938
BLENHEIM	1938 - 1939
HAMPDEN	1939 - 1941
MANCHESTER	1941
LANCASTER	1942 - 1945

The Squadron was given a bomber role and equipped with Hawker Audaxes and Avro Ansons. This was to get some of the aircrew trained before they were allocated the new Bristol Blenheim Mk1 medium bomber in January 1938. However, by the end of the year it had been decided by the Air Chiefs of the newly formed Bomber Command that No.61 Squadron should become part of No.5 Group (Bomber) and convert instead to the new Handley Page twin-engine bomber called the Hampden. The Squadron received its first Hampden Mk1 (L4103) on 17th February 1939 and eighteen days later became fully equipped with the aircraft type.

When World War Two broke out in September 1939 there was little for the Squadron to do for the first three months but train for the expected daylight bombing operations against German military targets.

On Christmas Day 1939 No.61 Squadron finally became operational by sending 11 Hampdens on an armed reconnaissance sortie over the North Sea. Nothing was sighted and the Squadron had to wait until 7th March 1940 before the first bombs were dropped in anger on an enemy destroyer steaming off the enemy coast. The following day the Squadron suffered its first aircraft operational loss when Hampden L4111 failed to return from a security patrol. Twelve days later a bombing raid was planned against the German sea-plane base at Hornum on the island of Sylt. This was in retaliation to a German raid on Scapa Flow naval base two nights before. This was Bomber Command's biggest operation of the war so far and the first one on a German land target. Five of the twenty Hampden aircraft taking part in the raid belonged to No.61 Squadron, of which four bombed the target and one aborted.

The official Strategic Bombing Offensive started at the end of the Phoney War period on 15th May. Squadron Hampdens continued to fly bombing operations from RAF Hemswell throughout 1940 and well into 1941. The most significant raid during this period was the first one against Berlin on the night of 25th-26th August 1940. The War Cabinet sanctioned this retaliation raid following German bombing raids against London and other English cities the previous night.

This raid was a strategic turning point in Bomber Command's campaign against German non-military targets. Between July and October 1940 the Squadron took part in the Battle of Britain by attacking German invasion barges being assembled at Channel ports and Luftwaffe airfields in France, Belgium and Holland.

In July 1941 the Squadron moved south to North Luffenham and while there began to re-equip with the new twin-engine Avro Manchester. This aircraft was capable of carrying a much bigger bomb load than the Hampden and was also better armed.

The Manchester should have been good for the Squadron, but unfortunately the aircraft's Rolls-Royce Vulture engines were totally unreliable and as a result caused the loss of many experienced aircrew. Despite this the Squadron managed to maintain an offensive against Germany during this difficult period and in October 1941 moved to RAF Woolfox Lodge.

The loss of shipping in the North Atlantic at the turn of the year increased and the fear was that the large German battleships would soon be joining the U-boats to cut off the UK's North American life line. In order to stop this happening Bomber Command was ordered by the War Cabinet to try and destroy at least two of the German capital ships while they were in the harbour of Brest on the French Atlantic coast.

The new year started with eight raids on this port resulting in little damage and few aircraft losses. The ninth raid took place on 31st January-1st February when a force of 72 aircraft from 5 Group flew over the English Channel and were duly given an unwelcome reception by the German coastal flak batteries. Bombing was not accurate, mostly due to a defensive smoke screen over the dock area. Three of 61 Squadron's nine Manchesters failed to return.

On the 12th February the Squadron was called upon with other squadrons to attack the German battle cruisers *Scharnhorst, Gneisenau* and the light cruiser *Prinz Eugen* during their Channel dash from Brest to the Baltic ports in northern Germany. During the voyage both *Scharnhorst* and *Gneisenau* were damaged and had to slow down after hitting sea mines laid by 5 Group Hampdens and Manchesters near the Fresian Islands a few nights earlier. Most of the bombers were unable to find the German ships in the poor weather conditions. The aircraft that did failed to hit their targets and suffered heavy casualties due to flak put up by the capital ships and the air cover supplied by the German coastal night fighter force of Bf110's.

Two days later the Air Ministry issued the famous Area Bombing directive to Bomber Command and on 22nd February the Command got a new boss, Air Marshal Arthur Harris. The front line bomber force he inherited consisted of 62 four-engine heavies and 484 twin-engine aircraft, including 20 troublesome Manchesters.

Meanwhile during the summer of 1941 the German Luftwaffe introduced a new night fighter control system code-named Himmelbett. In essence Himmelbett was a chain of defensive zones that stretched from north western France up to the German Baltic coast. Each zone was covered by a Würzburg ground to air radar unit to detect hostile aircraft and this information was fed into a control centre from which night fighters were directed to intercept any incoming RAF Bombers.

Such an interception took place over Holland at 00.32 hours on 26th March 1942 when P/O Hubbard's aircraft, Manchester L7518, QR-O Orange, was located and shot down by a Bf110 piloted by the German night fighter ace, Oberleutnant Helmut Lent of the II/NJG2 from Leeuwarden A/B. Only two members of the Manchester's crew survived the attack to become prisoners of war. At the same time as the German defensive reorganisation, Air Chief

Marshal (now Sir Arthur) Harris was bringing pressure on the Air Ministry to quicken the pace of re-equipping his front line squadrons with four-engined aircraft. This new generation of aircraft gave the squadrons a greater bomb carrying capacity, higher speed, longer range, increased reliability and crew safety. While other front line groups were building their four- engine bomber strength with the Stirling and Halifax, No.5 Group started re-equipping its squadrons with the highly rated Lancaster and in April 1942, much to the relief of its aircrews, No.61 Squadron converted to the new four-engine bomber.

At the beginning of May the Squadron moved from Woolfox Lodge to RAF Syerston in Nottinghamshire. This station had just re-opened as a No.5 Group heavy bomber base after having three concrete runways laid. The first operational sortie flown by the Squadron from their new home took place a few days later on 5th May 1942.

On the last night of the month the Squadron's Lancasters took part in Bomber Command's first Thousand Bomber raid against Cologne. Two nights later, 1st-2nd June, the thousand bomber force was again assembled, but this attack on Essen was not a success. Better results were obtained at the end of the month against the shipyard and Focke-Wulf aircraft factory at Bremen.

Shortly afterwards No.61 was loaned to Coastal Command to help its hard pressed squadrons cope with the U-boat menace in the North Atlantic. During this period the Squadron operated from RAF St.Eval in Cornwall. On the Squadron's first operation with Coastal Command, Lancaster R5724 QR-F Freddie captained by F/Lt P.R.Casement, became the first aircraft in Bomber Command to destroy an German U-boat at sea. However this diversion didn't last long and the Squadron were soon back on nightly sorties to Germany.

In October 1942 the Squadron Lancasters took part in the daring low level daylight raid on the Schneider factory at Le Creusot, near the German/Swiss border. The only casualty of the raid was Lancaster W4774 flown by S/L W.D.Corr of No.61 Squadron. He was part of the force briefed to attack the Montchanin power station which was situated a few miles away from the primary target. This he did at such a low level that his exploding bombs caused the aircraft to crash in the target area.

During the spring of 1943, No.61 Squadron played its part in the successful Ruhr and Hamburg bombing campaigns. The industrial Ruhr, nicknamed Happy Valley by the aircrews, was defended by a ring of heavy flak installations. This battle lasted four months from 5th March to 24th July and was successful mainly due the high flying Mosquito Pathfinders who marked the target with great accuracy using the new Oboe long range blind bombing system.

However the Happy Valley defences claimed 870 aircraft from Bomber Command's front line squadrons. The Battle of Hamburg, Operation Gomorrah, soon followed and is regarded as the most concentrated and successful series of raids carried out by Bomber Command during the war. This was again due to the accurate target marking by the Lancaster Pathfinder squadrons of No.8 Group. During the battle, the Pathfinder Target Illuminator aircraft were able to pinpoint targets more accurately by using the new short range H2S air to ground blind bombing equipment. They also dropped millions of silver paper strips, code named Window, to confuse the German radar.

When Albert Speer, the German Minister of Armaments, visited Hamburg and saw the damage caused by Operation Gomorrah he reckoned that another six similar raids against other German cities might end Germany's capacity to continue the struggle. Unfortunately Bomber Command was not strong enough to inflict such damage to cities deep inside Germany and so shorten the war.

On 20th-21st June 1943, five of No.61 Squadron Lancasters took part in operation Bellicose. This raid on Friedrichschaven in southern Germany was the first Bomber Command shuttle operation to Allied air bases in North Africa. It was also the first time the Master Bomber technique was used to control the bombers over the target area.

On 17th-18th August 1943 four of the Squadron Lancasters failed to return after taking part in the successful maximum effort raid against the V-2 rocket development and production sites at Peenemünde on the Baltic coast. It was also the first time German night fighters used their new Schräge Musik weapon. This lethal installation consisted of two upward-firing 20 mm cannon fitted behind the pilot's head in the cockpits of Bf110 and Ju88 aircraft. This enabled the night fighter pilot to approach a bomber unseen from below and attack it from very short range without using tracer ammunition. Shortly afterward it was rumoured throughout Bomber Command the Germans were using a new exploding anti-aircraft shell which gave the appearance of an aircraft exploding in the bomber stream. These explosions were nicknamed Scarecrows. What the aircrews were actually witnessing was the result of an attack by a night fighter fitted with this Schräge Musik weapon. Many of the No.61 Squadron aircraft lost during the winter of 1943-44 was by German night fighters fitted with this weapon.

Since taking over Bomber Command in February 1942, Air Chief Marshal Sir Arthur Harris had slowly built up his heavy bomber squadrons for a big offensive against Berlin and other important industrial targets deep inside German territory.

The first phase of the so called Battle of Berlin started on 24th August 1943 and ended seven months later on 31st March 1944. During this period the Squadron flew a total of 267 sorties in 20 raids on the Big City for the loss of 11 Lancasters. Only two of the missing aircrew survived to become prisoners of war. A typical raid during this period was the mission against the old town of Kassel on 22nd-23rd October 1943 where over one hundred industrial buildings were destroyed. Amongst these were aircraft factories producing the secret V-1 flying bombs. Unfortunately the price paid by Bomber Command was a high one with 43 (7.6%) of the attacking force failing to return. No.61 Squadron provided 15 Lancasters for this raid and suffered the loss of 3 aircraft (20%) due to night fighter activity. One of the missing aircraft, Lancaster W4279 QR-Z Zebra, was flown by the Squadron's commanding officer, Wing Commander W M Penman DFC AFC.

Victoria Cross:

On the night of 3rd November 1943, F/Lt William Reid's crew were briefed to take part in a raid on the Mannesmann steel works on the outskirts of Düsseldorf. While crossing the Dutch coast at 21,000 feet their aircraft, Lancaster LM360 QR-O Orange, was attacked by a Messerschmitt Bf110 night fighter from dead astern. Its cannon shells put the Lancaster's gun turrets out of action and shattered Reid's cockpit wind-screen. After confirming his crew were unscathed he decided to carry on with the sortie despite the bitterly cold slipstream entering the cockpit. Reid was himself wounded in the head, shoulders and hands. Soon afterwards the Lancaster was attacked again, this time by a single-engine Focke-Wulf 190. The enemy's fire raked the bomber from nose to tail, killing the navigator and fatally injuring the wireless operator. Although the situation was now dire, Reid's depleted crew continued with the operation and bombed the target some 50 minutes later.

After clearing the target area Reid managed to set a course for home by using the Pole Star and moon. With the assistance of the flight engineer and bomb aimer Reid managed to fly the damaged aircraft back to England before carrying out an emergency crash landing at RAF Shipdham in Norfolk.

For his superb courage and leadership F/Lt William Reid was awarded the Victoria Cross. The flight engineer Sgt James W.Norris was awarded the rare Conspicuous Gallantry Medal for his devotion to duty during the operation. Although injured himself during the second fighter attack, Norris took over the Lancaster's controls when his skipper drifted into unconsciousness during part of the return flight to England.

Similar acts of bravery, some unacclaimed, were enacted many times by Squadron aircrew during Bomber Command's five year bombing offensive against Nazi Germany.

F/L Reid's badly shot up Lancaster QR-O Orange after the Dusseldorf raid 3rd November 1943

Flt. Lt. William Reid V.C.

THE LONDON GAZETTE
14th December, 1943

Wounded in two attacks, without oxygen, suffering severely from cold, his navigator dead, his wireless operator fatally wounded, his aircraft crippled and defenceless, Flight Lieutenant Reid showed superb courage and leadership in penetrating a further 200 miles into enemy territory to attack one of the most strongly defended targets in Germany, every additional mile increasing the hazards of the long and perilous journey home. His tenacity and devotion to duty were beyond praise.

On 16th November 1943 at the start of Bomber Command's winter phase of the Battle of Berlin the Squadron moved from Syerston to the primitive wartime facilities of RAF Skellingthorpe near Lincoln. Two days later they flew the first of eleven operations to be carried out against Berlin during their initial two month stay at Skellingthorpe. They shared the airfield facilities with No.50 Squadron and as both squadrons were building up their operational strength it wasn't long before an acute accommodation problem arose. In order to alleviate the problem No.61 Squadron went on a three month detachment to RAF Coningsby on 12th January 1944.

During the Battle of Berlin, the Squadron took part in fifty-one major bombing operations against strongly defended targets inside Germany and suffered many aircraft losses to heavy flak and a very well organised Luftwaffe night fighter force. Although Bomber Command caused mass destruction of property and inflicted terrible suffering on the German people, they failed to bring about the German surrender that Sir Arthur Harris had hoped would result from this bombing campaign. It was an extremely hard fought battle and the cost to Bomber Command was high with 1,100 aircraft and 8,000 highly trained aircrew lost.

The Battle of Berlin finally ended with the disastrous Nuremberg raid on the 30th–31st March 1944 when ninety-five RAF heavy bombers were shot down over enemy territory and another fifteen crashed in England. The reason for such high aircraft losses was because senior planners thought there would be cloud cover over the route before the moon set. Even so crews were still briefed to fly a long outward leg of 265 miles through a well defended part of Germany past known night fighter beacons in bright moonlight. These radio beacons were used as night fighter holding areas until Luftwaffe ground controllers decided the direction of the bomber stream.

Nuremberg was a maximum effort raid and No.61 Squadron dispatched 14 Lancasters from their Coningsby base. The following morning only ten crews reported bombing the target, three aircraft returned with damage and two failed to return. Aircrew casualties amounted to 16 men killed and four wounded in returning aircraft.

Lancaster ME595 QR-R was flown by P/O Donald Paul and crew for this operation. As the aircraft flew past night fighter beacon Ida, near Cologne, on the outward leg, it was attacked by a twin engine Ju 88 night fighter. Over the next fifteen minutes vigorous corkscrewing by the pilot and good work by the gunners managed to stave off two further attacks. However during the defensive manoeuvres the aircraft had lost altitude and suffered severe damage to two engines that had to be shut down. Still loosing height and down to 10,000ft the skipper had no alternative but to get rid of his bomb load and turn for home. Later after throwing everything moveable out of the aircraft in order to maintain height and flying speed over the North Sea, Don Paul managed to land safely at RAF Manston.

Amongst the night's FTR (failed to return) casualties was Lancaster DV311 QR-P flown by S/L E H Moss DFC. Nuremberg was the crews 20th operation and they were regarded as the Gen Men or Old Sweats of the Squadron. However all the crew were killed when their aircraft were shot down by Hauptmann Rudusch flying a Me 110 night fighter near Rimbach NW of Fulda.

Another victim was veteran Lancaster R5734 QR-V piloted by Australian P/O J A Haste. The aircraft was detected by Major Rudolf Schoenert flying a Ju 88 night fighter fitted with Naxos aircraft location equipment. This device picked up H2S radar signals. The German night fighter followed QR-V for over half an hour picking up intermittent H2S signals from QR-V. The German pilot's persistence finally paid off when he saw his quarry heading for home at 20,000ft. Unseen he positioned his aircraft underneath the Lancaster and fired cannon shells from his Schräge Musik weapon into QR-V Victor's right wing tank. The Lancaster caught fire and crashed near Namur in Belgium. There were no survivors.

Another Squadron aircraft, QR-M Mickey The Moocher, ran into difficulties while flying over the North Sea towards the north Norfolk coast. It encountered stormy conditions and was struck by lightning on the front turret causing Aussie skipper P/O J A Forrest to lose control and the aircraft plummeted towards the sea. While in a blinded and shocked state the pilot ordered the crew to bale out while he tried to pull the aircraft out of the dive. Forrest managed to gain control again at an altitude of only 1000ft and immediately countermanded his bale-out order. Unfortunately it was too late to save the lives of the wireless operator and mid-upper gunner who had already parachuted into the sea.

Meanwhile, Lancaster R5856 QR-Q Queenie had just flown past the Otto night fighter radio beacon near Frankfurt, when it was raked by cannon fire from a Bf 110 and two Ju 88 night fighters. Despite suffering severe damage to his aircraft and with four badly injured crew members aboard, P/O Denny Freeman managed to return to England and crash land the aircraft at RAF Foulsham in Norfolk.

Although this was only his third operation P/O Freeman displayed great courage after the night fighter attack and was awarded an immediate Distinguished Flying Cross upon his return to Coningsby. Freeman's wireless operator F/S Leslie Chapman was awarded the Conspicuous Gallantry Medal for repairing his damaged radio and getting vital navigational radio fixes. Sadly both men died later while flying ops with other crews.

By the spring of 1944 Bomber Command aircrew knew they only had a one in three chance of completing a thirty bombing operations tour. Even so the young bomber crews continued to dice with the Grim Reaper night after night in the hostile skies of Western Europe.

P/O Denny Freeman DFC

F/S Leslie Chapman CGM

Lancaster R5856 QR-Q Queenie with Bomb Aimer F/S DG Patfield

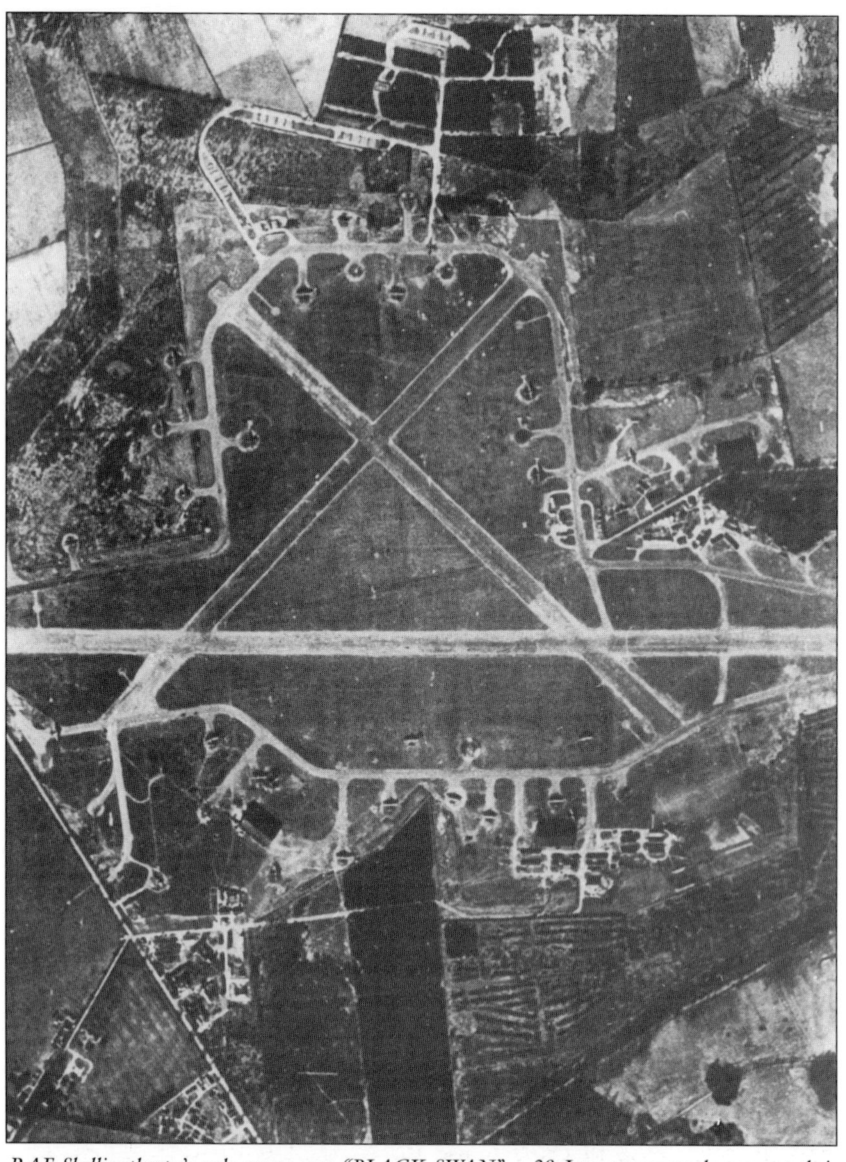

RAF Skellingthorpe's code name was "BLACK SWAN" – 29 Lancasters can be seen at their dispersals

CHAPTER 4

OPS ARE ON TONIGHT

Early in the day the Station's Commanding Officer would be waiting in the Operations Room for a teleprinter message from Group headquarters containing orders for the next bombing operation to be carried out by the squadrons on his bomber station. With him would probably have been the Wing Commander and Intelligence Officer.

Aircrew checked the notice boards in their Mess or Squadron office to see if their name was on the Battle Order for that night. Orderlies would also awaken aircrew asleep in their billets if they have been called upon to do consecutive night operations. Weather forecasts had to prepared by the Meteorological Officer and the Signals and Medical Officers were also notified about the impending operation.

Out on the Flight Lines:

Upon receipt of the Operation Orders the airfield became a hive of activity as the various ground staff trades set about their tasks to bring the Squadron aircraft to a state of readiness for the night's operation. Scores of airmen and WAAFs took a hand in getting every aircraft on the Squadron ready for the appointed take-off time. Operational aircraft stood up to severe punishment during the course of a bombing operation. Not only from normal wear and tear, but all too often aircraft returned with flak or night fighter cannon shell damage. Consequently its serviceability depended upon the work carried out by the Squadron ground staff. Each bomber aircraft had its own ground crew made up of men who were skilled in a particular job and headed by a corporal. He usually possessed the trade qualifications of Fitter One the highest grade of any trade in the Royal Air Force. Under his supervision were a crew of eight Aircraft hands (ACH) consisting of two Flight Mechanics (engines) and two Flight Mechanics (airframe) plus a Wireless Mechanic, Electrician, Instrument Repairer and Fitter Armourer.

Armourers line up an 8,000 lb Cookie with the Lancs bomb bay

Armourers steady the big Cookie while it is winched into position

During the winter months of 1943-44 No.61 Squadron had approximately twenty five Lancasters on strength and these aircraft were divided and maintained by two ground crew flights. Exercising general supervision over the ground crew on each flight was a Sergeant of each trade, who in turn was directly responsible to a Flight Sergeant who acted as technical adviser when difficulties arose.

When the ground crews reported at the Squadron hangar each morning, they were detailed to their duties, which generally meant a complete daily inspection of each aircraft.

After each operation the engine mechanics were fully employed in checking fuel pipe lines for security, inspecting magnetos, looking for leaks in the fuel, oil and coolant tanks and associated components. In addition, the variable-pitch airscrew had to be examined and tested for its full range of movement. This task was done while the engine was running. Oil pressures and the temperatures of oil and coolant were all checked together with the revolutions of the engines per minute. These, with an examination of the boost pressure, were only a few of the items that had to be noted before final clearance was given.

During this time the airframe mechanics were checking the freedom of movement of the controls and taking up slack if required. The hydraulic system of the undercarriage was looked into, tyre pressures and oil levels in air compressors were checked and the fabric and metal surfaces were carefully searched. These surfaces were closely scrutinised for damage and corrosion and then the entire aircraft was cleaned of all oil and dirt.

Meanwhile, the wireless mechanic tested the receiving and transmitting sets, accumulators were recharged, or coils replaced as necessary. The aerial wiring was followed through, and the system tested with a ground station. The aircraft's TR-1154-55 wireless sets were of great importance to the aircrew as the equipment had to be capable of receiving and sending vital signals that could help in an emergency to bring damaged aircraft safely home. All the various electrical installations were tested including bomb circuits, intercommunication (intercom) for the crew to speak from one post to another inside the aircraft. They were thoroughly tried out by the electrician and signal lamps, batteries and circuit fuses were all rigorously tested. The instrument repairer examined all the flying and navigational equipment and made sure it was in working order.

This was no small task in the general scheme of aircraft maintenance. There were engine speed indicators, directional gyros, rate of climb indicators, instruments showing angle of bank, compasses and air speed indicator, and others showing engine temperature and pressure gauges. Petrol bowser drivers also made sure that each aircraft had sufficient fuel in its tanks to complete the forthcoming operation safely.

Last, but certainly not least, the armourer tested the hydraulically operated gun turrets, cleaned all the machine guns, and saw that all bomb releases in the bomb bay were in full working order. It was also the Squadron armourers responsibility to provide the right bomb load to each aircraft and check that the bombs were properly housed and correctly fused, and that all safety devices were in position. When all these details had been attended to the respective tradesmen signed the maintenance Form 700 which stated that all equipment had been tested. This form was taken to the Flight Sergeant, who satisfied himself that all was correct before he too signed the certificate which immediately placed the aircraft as 'Ready for flight'.

Operations Staff:

During the day the Intelligence Officer gathered together all the information on file about the target for that night. Target information had been painstakingly collected over a long period in readiness for such an operation. At the briefing he would highlight enemy ground and night fighter defences and distinctive landmarks which would help pilots and navigators check their position en-route and over the target. To supplement all this information the I.O. contacted the Group Intelligence Officer to see if he had any fresh information about the target and enemy defences.

The Met Officer awaited a report from the latest Met Flight over enemy territory before putting together his weather forecast covering take-off, en-route, target area and return to base.

The bulk of the work in preparing the aircraft was carried out by the ground staff, but the aircrew nevertheless kept a sharp eye on the various tasks to see that nothing was left undone. If necessary an air test was carried out by the aircrew in order to check out the engines and various electrical and mechanical systems. The air gunners would also test their guns by firing hundreds of rounds at flame floats dropped into the sea. These flights were also part of the endless training an operational crew undertook to improve their chances of survival.

Because of operational losses and tour expired crews, the Squadron was made up of aircrews with varying degrees of operational experience. The successful aircrews, the Gen men of the Squadron, were the ones who had flown together many thousands of miles and had achieved a high level of understanding and trust in each others ability. This team spirit plus a lot of luck was essential if they were to survive a thirty operation tour.

The Briefing:

Prior to the main briefing, specialist briefings took place on Navigation, Bombing and Signals. At the appointed time the crews assembled in the operations room for the start of the main briefing, which covered all the important aspects of the operation.

The Squadron Commander would read out the Operational Order he had received from Group headquarters and then uncover a large wall map of western Europe showing the routes to be followed. This was neatly indicated by a long piece of coloured tape pinned across the map showing base to target and return routes. These routes had been carefully chosen in order to avoid flying over known heavily defended areas. A separate board listed the names of the pilots against the call-sign of each aircraft taking part in the raid. The take-off times for each aircraft and details of the kind of bombs loaded on the aircraft were also displayed. After his general overview of the operation, the Squadron Commander would also pass on any special instructions that he had received from Group Headquarters. The Flying Control Officer then briefed the crews about the runway in use for the operation and take-off procedures to be followed.

The Intelligence Officer then brought out his detailed maps to go over the route with the pilots, navigators and bomb aimers pointing out landmarks and drawing special attention to prominent features by which landfall could be recognised. Barrages and strong points in the enemy ground defences were indicated and the type of target indicators and route markers that would be used by the Pathfinder squadrons. Questions were answered, and any doubtful elements of his presentation were explained. He was followed by the Met Officer whose weather charts showed the weather conditions in the target area, the type of cloud that could be encountered en-route and the possibility of any ice or fog upon return to base in the early hours of the morning. Next, the Wing Commander gave advice on the operation. He had probably been over that part of enemy territory many times before. His words, based on his personal experience, were especially helpful to the sprog crews. The station Group Captain added a few words of encouragement, stressed the importance of the operation, wished the crews good luck, and the briefing was over.

The crews would still have a couple of hours before take-off. Some would go to their billets to try and relax while others would go to the mess for their pre-ops meal of bacon and eggs just in case they didn't get back in the morning.

Meanwhile the navigators still had to work out their courses based upon take-off times and target estimated time of arrival (ETA). Aircraft captains also had a number of last-minute jobs to do that could not be done until after briefing. Next they would meet in the aircrew locker room, change into their flying kit and collect their parachutes and safety equipment. Outside the lorries and buses lined up to take them out to their aircraft's dispersal.

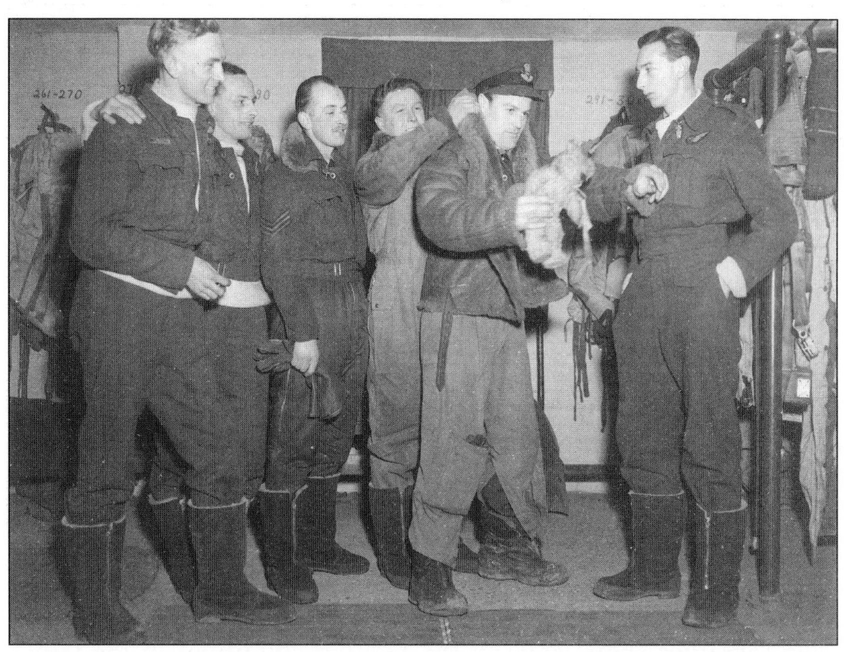

Squadron locker room at RAF Syerston 1943 - Don't forget the lucky mascot

Aircrew arrive at a distant dispersal

Crew walk over to their aircraft, RAF Syerston 30th July 1943

Crew of W4236 QR-K Kitty: F/Lt Hewish (B/A) Sgt Petts (N) Sgt Vanner (R/G) P/O Eager (P) Sgt Stone (W/Op) Sgt Sharrard (MUG) Sgt Lawrence (F/E)

Canadian P/O W.H.Eager about to start engines on W4236 QR-K Kitty

P/O Eager opens the throttles on QR-K for take-off to Hamburg 30th July 1943

Take-off:

The time arrived for the heavily laden aircraft to be made ready for take-off. An electrical starter trolley was wheeled out, rations are put aboard and emergency rations were stowed near the collapsible dinghy in case the aircraft had to be abandoned over water. Meanwhile the armourer gave a final check to bomb load and machine guns.

The crews arrived at their aircraft dispersal and made final checks around the kite, after which they carried out their individual rituals, a last minute cigarette or wetting the rear wheel for good luck. They boarded the aircraft and settled down in their crew take-off positions. Even then there could be a last minute scrub of the operation due to bad weather en-route or in the target area.

A Very light would be fired from the control tower signifying engine start-up time had arrived for the waiting bomber crews. With bomb doors closed and engines started each pilot tested his aircraft's controls, ran the engines and assured himself that everything was in order before leaving the dispersal.

Chocks were waved away and at the appointed time the pilot

taxied the aircraft to the perimeter track and joined other aircraft weaving their way to the holding point at the end of the runway. After receiving a Green on the Aldis lamp from the controller's caravan, each aircraft taxied onto the end of the main runway. The pilot applied the brakes, revved the engines, closed the throttles again before slowly revving the engines up again into a mighty roar. Brakes were released and the aircraft slowly moved forward gaining speed as it bounced on the undercarriage hydraulics under the weight of a full bomb and fuel load. This was a most critical time as the pilot concentrated to control the aircraft's tendency to swing to port due to the massive torque created by four Merlin engines at full power. The loss of power from one of the engines or a burst tyre could spell instant disaster for the crew. Eventually with most of the runway consumed it struggled free of terra firma. Then, with its undercarriage retracted the Lancaster quickly gained height and disappeared in the fading light. There may have been a non-stop run of over a thousand miles before it returned.

Once in the air, nothing more would be heard from the aircraft until the captain sent a coded message telling base that the mission had been completed. Only in an emergency would he break radio silence while over enemy territory.

The ground staff had not yet finished. The Flight Sergeant in charge of each Flight detailed a crew to stand by in readiness in case any aircraft had to return because of unforeseen circumstances. This was a rare occurrence compared with the number of sorties flown. Meanwhile, each aircraft was trimmed to climb up to their Bomber Stream operational height on the first leg of the route to the target. As the crews settled down they continually checked their aircraft for any mechanical or electrical faults which could prevent them from carrying out the operation.

The first dangerous obstacle the crews faced was the cold and forbidding North Sea. This stretch of water became a graveyard for many crews during the five year conflict. As the bomber stream crossed the enemy coast it was greeted by the pre-alerted enemy searchlights and heavy flak from the coastal batteries. While further inland the German night fighter squadrons had already been alerted by the Luftwaffe night fighter control centres, whose staff were busy trying to determine the route and eventual target of the incoming bombers.

As the bomber stream threaded its way between the flak and searchlight defences of the well protected German industrial cities, the night fighters would be already seeking their first victim of the night. Casualties would appear as a sudden explosion in the night sky or a fireball falling to earth.

Ahead the pilots and bomb aimers of the main force would see the route markers and later the red and green Target Indicators (TIs) dropped by the Pathfinder squadrons. The marked target area quickly became alive with roving beams of light from searchlight batteries and exploding shells from hundreds of heavy flak gun emplacements that encircled the city below.

Soon each aircraft would turn on its final approach towards the target and once committed the pilot had to fly the aircraft straight and level up to the aiming point. The bomb aimer at his bomb-sight gave final instructions to the pilot before releasing the bomb load on the target indicators and into the inferno far below.

During this perilous period, the rear and mid-upper gunners continued to keep a close lookout for fighters and possible collision with friendly aircraft in the crowded night sky. While, in his curtained office, the navigator busied himself working out a course for home.

Throughout numerous probing searchlights tried to seek out their aircraft and salvos of heavy flak shells reached up trying to destroy them. Even after the call "bombs gone" from the bomb aimer, the pilot had to keep the aircraft straight and level until the aiming point photographs had been taken. This was the most dangerous and nerve-racking period for the crew during the whole bombing run as aircraft became sitting ducks for the radar-controlled predicted flak batteries below. Once the photographs had been taken, the pilot quickly closed the bomb doors, executed a full boost turn away from the holocaust below, before diving into the comparative safety of the blackness beyond.

Bomber stream heads east over the North Sea

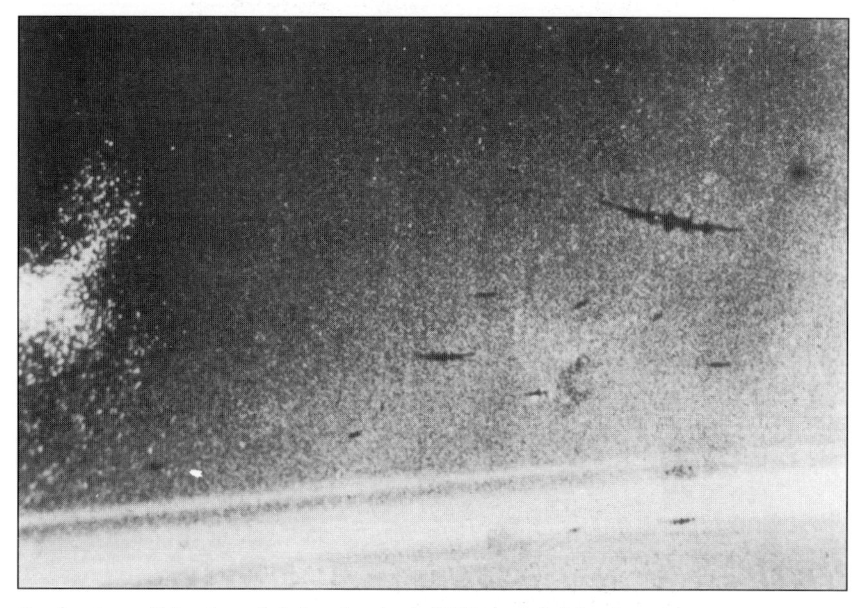

Bomber stream flying through flak and a cloud of 'Window' tinfoil strips

Pathfinder aircraft flying through heavy flak to release TIs over a German city

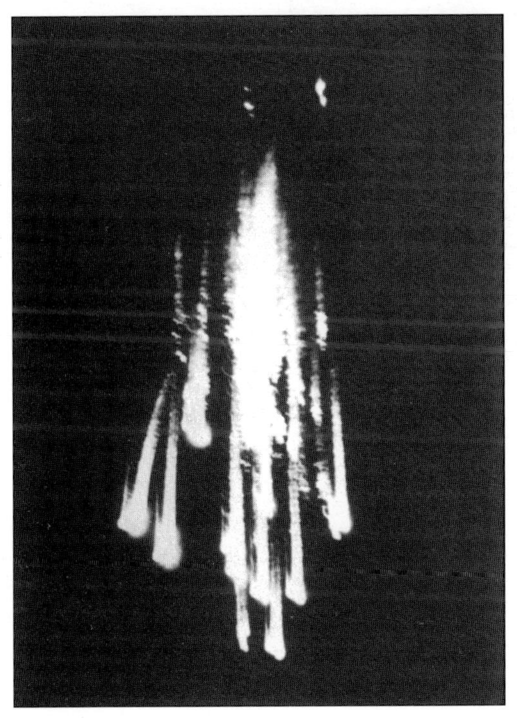

Cluster of Target Indicators (Christmas trees) mark the aiming point

Wild Boar Bf 109 pilot waits for take-off instructions

Radar equipped Bf 110 night fighters search for the raiders

Salvo from a German battery of 8.8 cm flak guns

The Return:

This was no less an anxious time for the crews. Every mile of the route home was fraught with danger, not only from enemy flak or prowling night fighters, but also from possible flak damage already sustained to a vital part in any one of the aircraft's complex systems.

Towards dawn the reception ground crews were ready and waiting. The faint hum of Merlin engines was heard in the distance - the first one was back - and work began again.

Aircraft would be given a landing number by Flying Control and circle the airfield until they were called to make their landing approach. Once down, each aircraft taxied to its own dispersal and the waiting ground crew. Tired from the night's stressful events the aircrew alighted from the aircraft and were welcomed back before being taken to a debriefing session with the Intelligence Officers on the success or failure of the night's operation.

After flying for many hours in a vibrating, cold and noisy aircraft over hostile territory, often in appalling weather conditions, sleep didn't come easy to many of the returning aircrew. Many would wonder why they volunteered for such perilous aircrew duties. Others would fall asleep happy with the thought that only the other crews got the Chop, and with a bit of luck they would soon complete their 30 bombing operations tour.

Lancaster returns safely to it's dispersal

Debriefing the crews

Start of Another Day:

Then the ground crew took over, the kite was theirs again. Each aircraft had a faults book in which the Captain noted any faults that occurred during the flight and had to be rectified before the next trip.

The Flight Sergeant and the senior NCOs in charge of each trade inspected the aircraft. Petrol, oil and coolant consumption was recorded so that the performance of the engines could be watched. Naturally, there were times when urgent repairs had to be made. Aircraft may have been hit by anti-aircraft fire or by night fighter attack. Sometimes they would return with serious damage to the airframe or control surfaces. Many returned with one or more engines out of action - but still they reached home. Damage was quickly assessed and a decision taken on whether the aircraft was repairable on the flight-line or whether specialist help was required. Photographs were taken for future reference.

If special jobs called for more expert workmanship than the flight personnel could give, there was a special flight of highly skilled workmen, representative of all trades, and called the Service Flight from which men could be called to deal with the emergency.

When all was finally completed, the aircraft went through the daily inspection and an air test prior to its next operational flight. Workmanship was of a highly skilled character and supervision was very strict. After all, the aircrews lives depended upon it.

CHAPTER 5

AIRCRAFT MAINTENANCE

LAC Ray Meredith (Flight Mechanic, Airframes)

Like many 18 year olds before me, I had high aspirations to be an RAF pilot. After failing my first aircrew selection board, I then received another letter from the Air Ministry implying that I might qualify to be a navigator, but again I failed. Undeterred, I pressed on in my pursuit of aircrew duties and was selected to train as a WOP/AG. Again I was thwarted after the aircrew medical revealed an eye sight defect. I was eventually offered the choice of Motor Transport - General Duties or Aircraft Maintenance. I chose the latter because I already had a technical background and it was reasonable to assume that I would have the chance to get airborne on air tests once I was established on a squadron. After 6 weeks initial training, I was posted to No 1 RAF School of Technical Training at RAF Halton. The technical training course at Halton was very intense, and involved a thorough understanding of metallurgy - control wires and splicing - hydraulics - pneumatics - control surfaces - tyres - metal and fabric repairs - riveting - monocoque construction - paint/cellulose finishes - nuts - bolts - rivets - salt bath operations for annealing, and not least aerodynamics.

This all fell within the scope of RAF airframe mechanics and fitters in 1943. After graduating from Halton I was posted to No.58 Maintenance Unit (MU) of 43 Group, based at Newark in Nottinghamshire. After a few weeks there I went on detachment to the No.5 Group bomber station at RAF Skellingthorpe, near Lincoln the home of No.50 and No.61 Squadrons.

Our crew from No.58 MU numbered about 20 in all, including six Polish airmen who proved to be excellent engineers. In their spare time they would transform odd bits of Perspex and metal into quite exquisite jewellery.

We were all billeted in wooden huts set amongst the pine trees opposite the main guard room. In the centre of each hut was a black coke fired stove mounted on a concrete base.

The floor was covered with brown inlaid linoleum and was sparsely furnished with twenty iron framed beds and small bedside lockers. The standard issue of three straw palliasses, two sheets, a pillow case and four blankets, was all we were given to provide comfort and keep out the bitterly cold winter weather.

We in 58 MU mainly worked in a large T2 hangar which could accommodate two Lancasters at a time. The hangar protected us from the weather and therefore we tended to work longer hours than the Squadron ground crew who were out on open dispersal sites. The NCO in charge of our flight was F/S Bishop from Birmingham. He delegated authority to Corporal 'Titch' Walker who I believe came from Nottingham. He was a really good worker, and a good chap to have around. He specialised in engines, as did fitters George Cole and Bert Hindle who both came from Lancashire. Ron Byard was also an engine fitter, and a former member of the RAF Regiment who had seen service in North Africa with the Desert Air Force. Ron was more fortunate than most married men at Skellingthorpe. His home was only three miles away at North Hykeham just the other side of the airfield, so his week-end passes had an enviable extension. Corporal Bill Haynes from the London area was also an airframe fitter. He was much older than the rest of us and a father figure to the younger members of the unit. We could always turn to Bill to sort out any technical problem, and be sure that what he said he was correct. Steve Pitt, another FMA, came from the Walsall area on the fringes of the Black Country and my home was in Birmingham, the engineering hub of the nation at that time.

Outside the hangar was our flight hut and technical stores. Most mornings aircraft could be seen in the midst an array of maintenance platforms, surrounded by numerous tool boxes, airmen for the use of. Suddenly the noisy compressors would be shut down and the area fall silent as two ladies with a Mobile Canteen came into view with char and wads for the boys. This service was run by the Sally Anne Church Army or some other charitable organisation and was always a welcome sight at mid-morning. After our mug of hot refreshing tea and a bun, it was back on one of the many platforms surrounding an aircraft on the apron or into the hangar to the cacophony of sound once again, so loud at times, that normal levels of speech were impossible. The scene inside the 58 MU hangar was typical of the work being carried out on other airfields throughout Bomber Command. Hangars were vast acoustic chambers mostly clad in corrugated metal sheeting with massive sliding doors at each end. A number of Windy drills at work and the sound of riveting which, was all done by hand I hasten to say, built up into a crescendo of sound which was deafening.

Inside, the aircraft stood in various stages of repair like patient horses waiting to be groomed. Some with trestles under every jacking point for tests on the undercarriage hydraulics and to allow checks on the angles of incidence of the mainplane and tailplane with a clinometer, to make certain the longitudinal spar was perfectly level.

The hangar floor area was kept spotlessly clean, while around each aircraft was a crisscross of hoses, supplying the Windy drills, interlaced with numerous power cables for inspection lights and electrical services. There were large rectangular oil trays placed on the floor beneath the engines and any other point where oil might have dropped or be spilt by accident. Protective covers were also draped over the main wheel tyres, to protect the rubber from being soiled, especially if work was being carried out on either of the inboard engines where oil spillage was often unavoidable.

From our domestic site early one winter morning in December 1943 after a heavy overnight frost I remember a peaceful Christmas scene. The pine trees were white with hoar and Lincoln Cathedral stood majestically on top of the hill with its spires glinting in the early morning sunshine. This tranquillity didn't last long, as in the distance the sound of Merlin engines could be heard as the station's Lancasters returned from a deep penetration raid over Germany. One by one the aircraft circled the airfield and made their landing approach. Just before touching down each pilot throttled back the engines before gliding over the threshold of the main runway. The fading sound of spluttering engines could be heard in the distance as each Lancaster came to the end of its landing run, only to be quickly replaced with the sound of the next aircraft home.

Some of the damaged aircraft had badly injured or dead aircrew aboard. Generally, returning aircraft automatically made their way to their own Squadron dispersal, irrespective of damage and casualties sustained. However in some cases, the station's ambulances met aircraft as it landed, to take-off the badly wounded to the station's sick quarters or the nearest hospital. I remember one Lancaster that was towed into the hangar after it had been in a mid-air collision the previous night. The starboard outer engine and its sub-frame was completely missing. The three bladed propeller sheared off and cartwheeled along the wing embedding itself in the fuselage, one blade missing the navigator by inches. The aircraft returned with the other two blades making their own Victory V sign behind the cockpit. Later, another aircraft returned without its main starboard fuel tank and the wing panelling underneath. It was another casualty of the crowded sky in the target area. In the upper skin of the wing, above the tank was found the perfect stamped out profile of a 500 lb GP bomb. A metal stamping press could not have done it better and it was a miracle that no one was killed. When we took delivery of aircraft with major damage it either taxied around to our hangar from its dispersal or was towed tail first by a Davy-Brown tractor. Sometimes the sight which met us on entering damaged aircraft was very upsetting. Remnants of a torn blood stained flying clothing were found and smears of dried blood around crew positions could be seen. These were constant reminders of the dangers faced by aircrew in the night skies high above Germany.

No.50 and 61 Squadron ground crews main task was to make the aircraft ready for the next operation by carrying out daily inspections, servicing and repairing minor operational damage. Each ground crew had a pride in and an affinity with their aircraft which ensured all the work done was of the highest standards.

However, it was The Flying 58th who were the surgeons at RAF Skellingthorpe. We attempted to make whole again the badly damaged aircraft that returned from bombing raids. How some of them got back, God only knows, they were in such a dreadful condition. A tail-fin and rudder missing, a whole engine gone, a fuselage or mainplane raked with cannon shells or shrapnel from anti-aircraft guns, and all too often the blackened and charred skin of the aircraft indicated there had been a fire on board. Sometimes we worked all day and night in order to get severely damaged aircraft into the air once more.

The Lancaster was made up of several sections and working from nose to tail along the fuselage, the D1 which formed the front gun turret and the cockpit was followed by the D2 centre section which housed the navigators table, the W/T and the flight engineer's panel. Behind that came the D3 section housing the mid-upper gun turret and radome beneath, and lastly came the D4 containing the flare chute, rear gun turret and leaflet chute. Each fuselage section was bolted together at two adjoining bulkhead frames with numerous nuts and bolts. The tailplane came in four sections including the elevators, the tail-fins and the rudders. The port and starboard mainplanes were made up of a leading edge, trailing edge and wing tip all bolted to the main section. Ailerons and flaps were then added along with four engine sub-frames, and the undercarriage. One of the most onerous tasks was the removal and replacement of the trailing edge to the mainplane. This involved undoing dozens of bolts holding it to the rear mainplane spar. Each mainplane was held in position to the centre-section with four huge high tensile steel bolts. For this operation the mainplane was suspended on two slings with a spreader bar between them. The replacement of the trailing edge was a nail-biting exercise for the operator of the Coles crane when lowering it into the correct position. Of all tools employed in the major surgery we performed on those aircraft, the Coles crane was the maid of all work and without it, many of the tasks would have been impossible.

The assembled aircraft was magnificent and a tribute to the makers A.V. Roe. It would be wrong of me not to mention the support we received from their repair depot at Bracebridge Heath near Lincoln. We, and the other airfields close by, were wholly dependant on their workforce for Lancaster spares. We could only work as fast as they could produce parts for our damaged aircraft. During 1944 there were often serious delays as the number of badly damaged kites increased and demand for spares exceeded supply. This resulted in frustrating delays, relieved only when a low loader arrived carrying large aircraft sections. We were indebted to the unsung heroes working long hours in the aircraft factories for these major replacement parts.

Throughout the day and night, Skellingthorpe airfield was alive as everyone worked away long hours at the task in hand. Our crew had no recognised period of work, we worked until the job was done. As a result, we were always the last to turn up for meals in the airmen's cookhouse. All too often the duty cook had placed our food in the ovens to keep it warm, and it was far less appetizing than it would have been a few hours earlier when it was fresh. It did however suffice to our need and we were too tired and too hungry to care.

Sometimes an operation target was changed at the last moment, which meant replacing the bomb load on the aircraft. Invariably it happened in the early hours of the morning when we were in a deep sleep after a long day. The station Tannoy would rasp out "all ranks immediately report direct to the bomb dump". If the target had been changed because of the weather you could bet your life it was pouring with rain or sleeting snow outside. Clad in whatever they had to keep out the wet and cold, an army of men would swarm towards the bomb dump on foot, bicycles, or if we were lucky aboard a 15 cwt truck. While out on the lonely dispersals the Squadron armourers worked like the clappers to replace the aircrafts bomb load.

Smoking inside the hangar was always strictly forbidden, understandably so, with so much 100 octane petrol vapour and dope thinners around. Indeed, we always had a 40 gallon drum full of petrol, with one end removed, in the hangar to wash our hands and tools of oil and grease. When a new drum was opened it also served as a cheap dry cleaning agency. We soaked our best blue uniforms in order to clean them ready for the next week-end pass. Hung out on coat hangars in the fresh air, they ponged a bit at first with petrol fumes, but a day out in the fresh air made the smell disappear, and the uniform when ready to wear was often far better than if it had been to a dry cleaners.

Whenever I managed to get a 48 hour weekend pass I would try and hitch a lift home to Birmingham. Most times all went well, but occasionally, while some drivers would drop me off at my destination, others no less well intentioned, would say "I've got to turn off here but something else may come along shortly". As a result I would be left stranded in some small village miles away from my main route home with the hours of my precious long weekend pass ebbing away. On the other hand travelling by train from Lincoln to Birmingham was quite an experience too. After waiting on a cold and drafty station platform the train would arrive packed full of servicemen. On main line trains the situation was even worse. I was lucky if a standing space could be found in the corridor, nevermind a seat and it was not uncommon to see someone sleeping on a carriage luggage rack.

At Skelly the personnel were a mixed bag of Brits, Canadians,

Australians, New Zealanders and 'Free' European Nationals, of all ages. The youngest Lancaster skipper on the Squadron was only just 20 years of age. Even so, he was deemed old enough to fly a powerful highly technical machine with a gross weight of 60,000 lb. In addition he had the burden of being responsible for the safety of his crew.

I will never forget the sound and smell of Merlin engines being started up and the scenes of activity in the various dispersals as the ground crews fussed over their aircraft.

When dusk approached we would see various types of vehicles travelling hither and thither to distant dispersals dropping the crews off by their aircraft. On the dispersal nearest to us, the aircrew would be seen sitting around on the grass smoking and chatting.

As take-off time approached they stubbed out their cigarettes, picked up their parachutes and threw them inside the aircraft. One by one they climbed aboard through the rear starboard doorway and would be lost from sight as each took up his crew position inside the aircraft. The pilot, sliding back the cockpit window on the port side, would give instructions to the ground crew to proceed with engine start up. With all four engines performing correctly chocks would be waved away followed by a hiss of escaping air as the brakes were released and the aircraft slowly moved out from the dispersal to join others of the Squadron on the perimeter track and then forward in single file towards the main runway. When his turn came each pilot would turn his aircraft onto the runway, apply the brakes, rev and clear all four engines, then throttle down again to a tick-over, awaiting a green light from the Flying Control caravan. Once the runway was clear, the controller's green Aldis lamp would flash at the waiting aircraft. This was always greeted by a loud cheer from a large group of off-duty personnel that had assembled nearby to wave good luck to each aircraft. As throttles were advanced the ensuing power generated by the four Merlins produced a sound that drowned all conversation and once the brakes had been released the aircraft slowly rolled forward down the runway before gaining speed in a series of gentle bounces under the weight of the heavy bomb load. Three quarters of the way down the runway the aircraft slowly rose into the air and with undercarriage retracted, quickly disappeared into the failing light on the first leg of its nocturnal operation.

After the last aircraft had clawed its way into the air and departed with the sound of its laboured engines fading away, the airfield fell strangely silent. Rural tranquillity descended once again on the surrounding woods and fields and as the group of WAAFs and airmen strolled back to their billets, rabbits came out of hiding and scurried across the main runway before disappearing once again into the long grass that edged this great expanse of concrete. While in the distance ground crews could be seen tidying the dispersals in readiness for their aircraft's return or cycling around the perimeter track to the cookhouse for their evening meal. Some of the aircraft would not return from the night's operation, but of those that did, it was inevitable that one or two would suffer severe airframe damage and would become No 58 MU's patients in the next morning.

Manchester L7477 QR-N damaged during attack on German Fleet 12th February 1942

No.61 Squadron Inspection and Repair Section at Skellingthorpe Lancaster ME596 QR-H went missing on the 12th August 1944 Rüsselsheim raid

RA593 QR-P with "B" Flight at RAF Skellingthorpe March 1945

CHAPTER 6

AIRCREW VOLUNTEER

P/O A 'Nobby' Clark DFC

About 125,000 aircrew flew operations with Bomber Command during the bombing campaign against Italy and Germany during World War Two. The following is a summary of my RAF service between 1940-46 and is typical of those who volunteered and were accepted for aircrew duties.

May 1920
I was born at the village of Thorney, near Lincoln. After attending the village junior school I gained a scholarship to a grammar school. In September 1931 I started senior school education at the City School in Lincoln and after passing the School Certificate I continued at school to take the examination for entry into the Civil Service.

June 1938
I started work in the Civil Service for the Board of Control and my first job was at Rampton State Institution near Retford in Nottinghamshire. I continued working there until early August 1940.

25th May 1940
Just after my twentieth birthday I registered for service with the Armed Forces and volunteered for RAF aircrew duties.

4th July 1940
I successfully passed a medical examination at the Newport Drill Hall in Lincoln, and after a short interview was provisionally put down for Wireless Operator/Air Gunner.

7th August 1940 RAF Cardington
Further instructions and a railway travel warrant soon followed and

I went to RAF Cardington near Bedford for an Aircrew Medical and Selection Board. I passed the medical and was selected for training as a Pilot.

On 9th August my group was told that we would be drafted into the RAFVR (Royal Air Force Volunteer Reserve) and this would take effect from 12th August. This was all rather sudden and I needed time to clear my desk at Rampton. I managed to get four days special leave but had to report back to Cardington by 20.00 hours on Thursday 15th August.

16th August 1940

On this day the Battle of Britain was in full swing with the Luftwaffe bombing the RAF fighter airfields in the south of England and there were numerous invasion scares. The recruit intake I was with stayed fourteen days at Cardington for a series of inoculations and some basic training and then went up to Blackpool for another eighteen days of square bashing. Following this, we were split into small parties and sent to many different camps.

Our group of eight were sent down to a Barrage Balloon Centre at Ely near Cardiff where we spent fifteen days doing general duties. Then three of us were posted to RAF Scampton of all places - only eight miles from my home! The remaining five were all posted to the Royal Air Force college at Cranwell.

While at Scampton we were put on Station Defence duties, against possible attack by German parachutists. However, after ten days we were on the move again. This time to Babbacombe, Torquay where we joined hundreds of other aircrew recruits and after further aptitude tests we were split into groups of fifty and posted to different Initial Training Wings (ITWs) to start on the Pilots Course. I was posted to No 7 ITW at Newquay.

October 1940 No.7 Initial Training Wing, Newquay

After ten weeks of intensive training, we had exams which all but one of our squad passed. We were then sent on seven days leave over the Christmas period and on our return we were split up into smaller groups.

January 1941 No.22 EFTS Marshals Airfield Cambridge
On 24 January, my group was posted to No 22 Elementary Flying Training School, Cambridge where we continued Pilot training in Tiger Moth aircraft.

In mid-March I suffered a big setback in achieving my ambition to fly with the RAF when I failed the test to fly solo and was immediately taken off the Pilots course.

25th March 1941 No.10 Radio-Telegraphy Signals School, RAF Blackpool
Along with other failed pilots, I re-mustered for training as a Wireless Operator/Air Gunner and was posted to No.10 Signals School. After twelve weeks of intensive Morse Code training I managed to achieved the required speed of sending and receiving 12 words per minute and, with other successful trainees, was given two weeks leave and posted for further training.

18th July 1941 No 2 Signals School, RAF Yatesbury
By the end of the three month technical training course our Morse speed had increased to 18 words per minute. The course finished on 7th October and we all received our Wireless Operator (Sparks) badges. Shortly afterwards we were told there would be a delay before we could continue our aircrew training so we were given two weeks leave and posted from home to various RAF stations to gain experience as ground wireless operators.

24th October 1941 RAF Market Drayton
After a few days at Market Drayton, two of us volunteered for a posting to the RAF School of Technical Training at Morecambe where the camp's Signals Scction not only served the training school but also the nearby WAAF Depot. I remained at Morecambe until June 1942, living and eating in a civilian billet.

June 1942 Aircrew Wing of No 2 Signals School, RAF Yatesbury
After an eight month delay I was at last posted back to Yatesbury to resume training for aircrew duties. From mid-June until mid-July we were instructed in the use of wireless equipment, both on the ground and in the air. We flew in Dominie and Proctor aircraft.

27th July 1942 No. 1 Air Gunnery School, RAF Pembrey, South Wales

We received instruction on firing .303 Browning machine guns and the operation of various types of aircraft gun turrets, both on the ground and in the air. The aircraft used were twin-engine Blenheims. At the end of our course, we received our Airgunner's badge and were promoted to Sergeants.

September 1942 No.25 Operational Training Unit, RAF Finningley

Our first and most important task at Finningley was to get organised as a crew of five flying in Wellington III aircraft to carry on training in our different trades. Our crew as follows:

Pilot	Sgt Ward Parsons, RCAF from Cayuga, Canada
Navigator	Sgt Bob Dyson, RAFVR
Bomb Aimer	Sgt Frank Poole, RAFVR from Weston-super-Mare
Wireless Operator	Sgt Nobby Clark, RAFVR from Thorney, Lincoln
Rear Gunner	Sgt Danny Towse, RAFVR from Kilham, Bridlington

After eight weeks of practice in navigation, bombing, gunnery and radio, including almost 100 hours flying Wellingtons, day and night, we moved on to convert to heavier bombers.

January 1943 No.1660 Heavy Conversion Unit, RAF Swinderby

For one day, we were posted to RAF Wigsley, which was only one mile from my home, but by the end of the day, we were sent over to the parent station in RAF Swinderby, eight miles away. Here we picked up a flight engineer and another gunner to make our crew up to seven:

Mid-Upper Gunner	Sgt George Isaacs, RAF from Hornchurch, Essex
Flight Engineer	Sgt Fred Mullins, RAF from Bristol

After some 13 hours on Manchesters and a further 16 hours on Lancasters, we had finished the course and were posted to No.61 Squadron, No 5 Group Bomber Command at RAF Syerston, near Newark.

February 1943 No.61 Squadron, RAF Syerston

Of all the squadrons in Bomber Command that we could have been posted to, No.61 suited me fine because the main feature of their Squadron badge was the Lincoln Imp and as I went to school in Lincoln it seemed a good omen! It was to be three weeks before we did our first operational sortie together but during that period I did four ops with two other crews as their wireless operators were sick. Once we started operations as a crew most of our sorties were flown in Lancaster W4900 QR-Q Queenie to targets in the Ruhr valley in Germany. We also went once to Berlin and three times to northern Italy during our tour.

By 14th June 1943 we had over twenty-five ops behind us and were considered by the Sprog crews to be Gen Men and one of the most experienced crews on the Squadron. As a result we, with four other seasoned crews, were temporarily taken off operations to carry out a series of flying exercises prior to taking part in a special operation called Operation Bellicose.

Lancaster W4900 QR-Q Queenie at RAF Syerston in July 1943

Maison Blanche, Algeria - 22nd June 1943 Standing L-R Danny Touse (RG) George Isaacs (MUG) Bob Dyson (N) Nobby Clark (W/Op) Sitting L-R Frank Pool (BA) Fred Mullins (F/E) and Ward Parsons (P)

OPERATION BELLICOSE

This took place on 20th-21st June 1943 when sixty Lancaster crews, four Pathfinders from 8 Group and fifty-six from 5 Group heavy bomber squadrons, were briefed to make a precision attack on the old Zeppelin works at Friedrichshaven on the shores of Lake Constance near the German-Swiss border. This factory made Würzburg radar sets which played an important part in locating British bombers flying through the defensive night fighter interception boxes in France.

The raid employed two new bombing procedures. The first was the appointment of a Master Bomber (Group Captain L.C. Slee), to control the main force in the target area. The second, was to fly to Allied bases in North Africa after the raid to confuse the German night fighter defences in France.

We, in Lancaster W5002 QR-L and four other Lancs of No.61 Squadron, took off from RAF Syerston at around 21.45 hours and headed south over East Anglia at the start of a five hour flight across France and southern Germany to the target area.

While flying over France the Master Bomber's aircraft developed engine trouble and his deputy, Wing Commander G.L. Gomm of

No.467 Squadron, took over the operation.

The weather at the target was clear, with Lake Constance and surrounding area bathed in bright moonlight, which enabled the Pathfinders to place their markers very close to the target.

The method of attack was in two parts. The first wave of bombers dropped their bombs on the target indicators laid down by the Pathfinders and the second wave was briefed to make a time and distance run from a prominent point on the shore of the lake to the estimated position of the factory.

Both attacking elements had been briefed to bomb visually from a height of between 5000-10,000 feet. Unfortunately the flak and searchlight defences were more active than expected so W/C Gomm ordered the bombers to climb to the safer height of 12,000 feet before attacking.

QR-L arrived in the target area at about 02.45 hours and we were immediately ordered to circle the area to gain some height. Our debrief entry in the Squadron log for that night states:

P/O Parsons identified the target visually and being at the incorrect height on receiving instructions to bomb, attacked later from 12,000 feet.

The aiming point photograph showed: **Roads and railways, plotted at the eastern end of Friedrichshaven.**

After the Lancasters had completed their bombing runs they flew south over the French Alps and Mediterranean to North Africa for a landing at either Maison Blanche or Blida airfields. Before leaving Syerston we had been briefed that weather conditions at these Algerian airfields in the early morning would not present any problems. However, when we arrived over Maison Blanche at about 1,200 feet we could only get fleeting glimpses of the runway as banks of low mist drifted across the airfield. There were already a number of aircraft in the circuit and pilots were continually calling the tower for permission to land, as fuel was getting short after ten hours in the air.

Instead of calling each aircraft down in turn, all they got back from the American controller was "Ship on the approach now, come on in, the runway's right below you". This confusion resulted in everyone attempting to get down at the same time. Even after landing the danger from collision was not over. As we slowed down at the end of the runway, Danny Towse, our rear gunner shouted over the intercom "For God's sake Skip get off the ------- runway quick, there's another kite coming up fast behind", or words to that effect!

Maison Blanche was a primitive desert airstrip and while there we all lived under canvas. However to ease the boredom we did managed to squeeze in a visit to the city of Algiers. Quite a change from our usual night out in Newark.

On the 23rd June 1943, fifty-two of the Lancasters that had bombed Friedrichshafen were bombed up and the aircrews were briefed to attack the oil depot at the northern Italian port of La Spezia. After completing the operation the crews were instructed to return to their home bases in England. Eight of the aircraft that bombed Friedrichshafen remained in North Africa for maintenance.

We took off in QR-L at 20.05 hours and after a one and a half hour flight over the Mediterranean we arrived off the Italian coast just south of the target area. In the distance the skipper saw a target indicator cascading down over the target and quickly turned on our bombing run.

Our debrief entry in the Squadron log for this attack records the following:

P/O Parsons saw one green marker and after identifying the bay visually, bombed 500 yards north of an oil fire from 11,250 feet at 21.33 hours.

Once clear of the target area we headed north-west over the Maritime Alps and five hours later, after an uneventful flight over France, landed safely back at RAF Syerston at 04.37 hours. The new bombing procedures tried during Operation Bellicose were deemed successful. In addition, when reconnaissance photographs were examined they showed that 10% of the bombs hit the target factory and many of the near misses destroyed other industrial premises.

By flying on to North Africa after the raid the bomber force confused the German night fighters that were waiting for them to return directly to England. As a result there were no Lancaster losses during either part of this operation.

My crew's last two ops were both to Gelsenkirchen, the first on 25th June and the second on 9th July. The latter was my 30th and last sortie of my operational tour and was destined to end in tragic circumstances. Shortly after we had bombed the target, we ran into heavy flak and our navigator, Bob Dyson, was hit by the only fragment of shrapnel that penetrated the fuselage and he died shortly afterwards. We headed west for home and by using radio aids and a bit of rough navigation by the second Bomb Aimer, whom we had on board for his introduction to ops, our skipper got us safely back to RAF Manston in Kent. We returned to our base at Syerston on 11th July. Two days later the Squadron Commander informed us that it had been decided our tour of operations had been completed and we would shortly be posted as Instructors for training new aircrew.

My Log Book lists the following targets during my tour of operations with No.61 Squadron:

Date	Target	Bomb Load	Ops No	A/C Captain
February 1943				
11	Wilhelmshaven	Usual	1	F/S Cockshott
14	Milan	Arson	2	F/S Cockshott
25	Nuremburg	Usual	3	Sgt Dundas
26	Cologne	Usual	4	Sgt Dundas
27	East Frisians	Gardening	5	Sgt W Parsons
March 1943				
4	Kattegat	Gardening	6	Sgt W Parsons
22	St Nazaire	Arson	7	Sgt W Parsons
29	Berlin	Usual	8	Sgt W Parsons
April 1943				
3	Essen	Usual	9	Sgt W Parsons
4	Kiel	Usual	10	Sgt W Parsons
8	Duisburg	Usual	11	Sgt W Parsons
9	Duisburg	Usual	12	Sgt W Parsons
11	Bay of Biscay	Gardening	13	Sgt W Parsons
13	La Spezia (Italy)	Usual	14	Sgt W Parsons
April 1943				
14	Stuttgart	Abnormal	15	Sgt W Parsons
16	Pilsen	No Ball	16	Sgt W Parsons
20	Stettin	Usual	17	Sgt W Parsons
May 1943				
4	Dortmund	Usual	18	Sgt W Parsons
12	Duisburg	Abnormal	19	Sgt W Parsons
13	Pilsen	No Ball	20	Sgt W Parsons
23	Dortmund	Usual	21	Sgt W Parsons
25	Düsseldorf	Usual	22	P/O W Parsons
27	Essen	Usual	23	P/O W Parsons
29	Wuppertal	Usual	24	P/O W Parsons

Date	Target	Bomb Load	Ops No	A/C Captain
June 1943				
11	Düsseldorf	Plumduff	25	P/O W Parsons
12	Bochum	Plumduff	26	P/O W Parsons
20	Friedrichschafen	Usual	27	P/O W Parsons
	Landed in Algeria			
23	La Spezia	Abnormal	28	P/O W Parsons
	Returned to Syerston			
25	Gelsenkirchen	Plumduff	29	P/O W Parsons
July 1943				
9	Gelsenkirchen	Plumduff	30	P/O W Parsons

Bomb Load Code:

Usual	=	1 x 4000 lb Cookie plus 12 Small Bomb Carriers (SBCs loaded with 24 x 30 lb or 236 x 4 lb incendiaries)
Arson	=	14 SBCs with incendiary mix up to a total weight of 14000 lb
No Ball	=	1 x 4000 lb Cookie plus 500 lb or 1000 lb GP
Plumduff	=	1 x 4000 lb Cookie plus 4 x 500 lb and 12 x SBCs
Abnormal	=	8 x 1000 lb GP
Gardening	=	Air/Sea mine laying sortie. 5 x 1500 lb mines

Note: The bomb load mix and total weight depended upon the type of target and the amount of fuel required to carry out each operation.

So ended our time together as a Lancaster crew with No.61 Squadron at Syerston. Returning from our end of tour leave, we learned that Bob Dyson and I had both been commissioned as Pilot Officer on 12th May 1943. We were also informed about our postings to various training units.

Our crew postings were as follows:
P/O W.Parsons, P/O A.Clark, Sgt G.Isaacs and Sgt Towse to report to No.17 Operational Training Unit (OTU) at RAF Silverstone on 23rd July 1943.
F/S F.Poole to report to No.16 OTU on 23rd July 1943
Sgt F.Mullins to report to No.81 OTU on 23rd July 1943.

23rd July 1943 No.17 Operational Training Unit, RAF Silverstone

After about three weeks the four of us were posted over to Silverstone's satellite airfield, RAF Turweston. We were soon all involved in giving operational flying instruction to trainee aircrew in old war-weary Wellingtons. Shortly afterwards I was made Signals Officer for B Flight.

On 14th September 1943, all the surviving members of our crew were informed that they had been awarded a decoration for completing a successful tour of bombing operations with No.61 Squadron. Ward Parsons, Bob Dyson and myself received the DFC, Danny Towes, Fred Mullins, Frank Poole and George Isaacs the DFM.

In the spring of 1944 Sgt Danny Towes and F/S Frank Poole went back to do a second tour of operations. Sadly both were lost on ops shortly afterwards, Danny was killed in action over Caen in Normandy and Frank died in a raid on Narvik in Norway.

In March 1944, our ex-skipper F/O Ward Parsons DFC, was posted to an all Canadian OTU at Gamston near Retford and in August 1944 our Mid-upper Gunner George Isaacs was also posted for a second tour of ops. This time with No. 223 Squadron, 100 Group at RAF Oulton in Norfolk.

Demob and Demand

I remained at RAF Turweston until it closed down in late 1945 when we returned to the parent station at RAF Silverstone. I remained there until March 1946 when I went on demob leave until my discharge on 8th May 1946.

A few months later I received a letter from the Air Ministry requesting the return of the Italian Star medal I had received for taking part in bombing raids against Italian targets. The only explanation I received was that the criteria for the award had been reconsidered.

Lancaster LN274 QR-F Skellingthorpe, L-R: W Dixon (W/Op) G Wilkie (RG) R Wake (B/A) W Burns (P) T Croaley (N) L Taylor (F/E) G Stokes (MUG)

Flight Commander S/L Beard with crew and ground staff of QR-G February 1944

CHAPTER 7

BAPTISM OF FIRE

Sgt C.J.'Jeff' Gray

With my crew, I reported to RAF Syerston in October 1943 to join No.61 Heavy Bomber Squadron, with very little idea of what lay ahead. We were, however, full of youthful exuberance and confident that we came with a good report from our instructors at the Operational Conversion Unit (OCU). Why else would they have cut short the final cross country stages and packed us off to a Squadron?

Our new Commanding Officer seemed unimpressed with us. "Shortage of Lancaster aircraft at the OCU might be nearer the mark for your early arrival" was his comment. Followed by the statement that he would not allow us to commence flying operations until we had made good our shortfall in flying time in Lancasters. However, he would find us an easy target with which to start our operational tour. This promise, was not, as it turned out, a simple one to discharge in the winter of 1943 while serving in a front line squadron of Bomber Command.

A few days later a distressing experience awaited us. The whole station was ordered on parade to witness some poor wretch being stripped of his rank and flying badges. It seems he had had enough and decided to go home. He made no attempt to run away, he simply went home. The Military Police brought him back to be disgraced in front of comrades. If we had been under any illusions as to the realities of the course on which we were now embarked, we were thus shortly disabused.

Then from Bomber Command Headquarters came the call for Maximum Effort from all bomber stations and we found ourselves briefed with the others for Berlin. So much for the CO's easy target. As we waited inside the aircraft for the time to start engines, I noticed with growing anxiety, the gathering fog shrouding the dispersal. On this still unfamiliar airfield, my first concern had to be finding the way out of the dispersal to the main runway. Then, much to my relief, a white Very light went up from the control tower signifying recall. The operation was scrubbed. We handed back the flying rations including the much prized chocolate bar. It was then I noticed we were the only ones to do so, one small lesson learnt. We returned to our programme of cross country flights. There was one consolation in all this. The Syerston base was only a few miles from Nottingham, famed throughout the RAF for its pretty girls, the fairest of the fair. Between the training flights and the 'promised' easy Target, hopefully there would be other delights.

Geoff Ward and I were rostered separately for our supernumerary flights. It was the custom then to treat the navigator and pilot of sprog crews to a trip with an experienced crew. The target was Düsseldorf, the date 3rd November 1943. My experienced crew were about mid-tour. To my surprise they spent a lot of time weaving about. This seemed particularly hazardous in the dark within a stream of bombers although I had heard there were those who favoured such a technique. As we approached the target the weaving continued. I could only guess that the defenders had resorted to a box barrage, each anti-aircraft shell bursting to leave a puff of black smoke which hung suspended in the night sky, the gaps between growing ever smaller. They showed up clearly in the glow of incendiary fires from below. At any moment I expected the pilot to straighten up in preparation for the bombing run but no, with the bomb aimer complaining the weaving continued. Then, more extraordinary still, we broke away, turning left across the bomber stream, then back the way we had come for a second approach. I must say I was most impressed by the cool and steely behaviour of the whole crew throughout this manoeuvre although I could not quite suppress the thought that it might have been better if they had got it right the first time round.

My navigator, Geoff, being a somewhat phlegmatic Yorkshireman, found nothing remarkable to report from his trip. But one member of No.61 Squadron, F/Lt William (Jock) Reid, most certainly did. Badly shot up by a night fighter on the way in, he persisted in bombing the target and made it home with his crew dead and dying about him. For his valiant effort that night he was awarded the Victoria Cross and his flight engineer, James Norris, the even rarer Conspicuous Gallantry Medal.

During this era, the senior officers of No.61 Squadron were much given to the press on regardless, stiff upper lip school of thought. So much so, that the Squadron records at the Public Records Office make no mention of Jock's VC, only a pencil entry added years later draws attention to his courage and determination. After recovering from his injuries Jock was poached by No.617 Squadron (The Dam Busters) where his Scottish tenacity was appreciated.

The CO's long awaited easy trip came up a week later on the 10th November 1943. The Squadron was part of a No.5 and 8 Group force briefed to bomb the entrance to the railway tunnel at Modane in the French Alps. Through this tunnel ran the main rail link into Italy.

As a spog (new) crew we didn't have a regular aircraft of our own so we had been given Lancaster EE176 QR-M Mickey the Moocher for this operation.

After getting the green light from the control caravan we turned onto the main runway. As we moved forward I felt at last we were an operational crew. Unfortunately my inexperience almost caused a disastrous ground loop. I wasn't used to the slow acceleration of a fully loaded Lancaster and I opened up the engines too soon before I had full rudder control. Slowly, but inexorably, we began to swing to port. It was decision time, I slammed the throttles shut and we ground to a halt. The crew were a little shaken up but otherwise ok so I decided the best thing to do was to try again. We quickly turned left off the runway, over the grass and passed very close to the Control Tower and rejoined the queue of aircraft for a second attempt. With McCulloch, my flight engineer, complaining about the engine coolant temperature going off the clock, we took another green light from the caravan and this time, making no mistakes, we lumbered off into the night.

The weather over France was perfect and by following the railway track the undefended target was easy to find. However the Pathfinder marking was slightly beyond the target but because of the usual raid creep back 200 Lancaster crews brought back photographs to show that their bombs fell within one mile of the aiming point. This raid resulted in the railway yard and tunnel being severely damaged thus preventing war materials getting through to the German army in Italy.

Ron Jones our Bomb Aimer said our run up to the target was perfect and he felt our bombing result would be good. After such an almost disastrous start to the operation everyone wanted to prove our worth to the Squadron CO.

As it turned out Ron was right and a week later Air Vice-Marshal Cochrane sent us his congratulations along with an aiming point photograph. We decided to keep quiet about our bombing success at Modane when talking to our peers and if ever I inclined to immodesty, my crew quickly reminded me of the row of ashen faces on the control tower balcony as our Lancaster hurtled passed. A few days later the whole Squadron was on the move to its new home at RAF Skellingthorpe. We packed our few possessions, waved goodbye to Nottingham and climbed aboard Lancaster QR-G George for the short hop across to Skellingthorpe. Never mind, they said, in Lincoln there are lots of pubs with lots of beer and the girls are just as pretty as the lace making girls of Nottingham.

All of which was probably true, but they forgot to mention that Lincoln was surrounded by at least ten other bomber stations and swamped by young men in blue.

Soon the long dark winter nights came upon us, the moon faded and Berlin, "The Big City", awaited our coming.

Jeff Gray and crew flew their tour of bombing operations with No.61 Squadron during the winter months of 1943-44 from RAF stations Syerston, Skellingthorpe and Coningsby.

As his tour progressed he witnessed a great uneasiness amongst the Squadron's aircrew as the German flak defences and night fighters gained the upper hand and reaped an ever increasing harvest of heavy bombers.

By the end of the so called Battle of Berlin in March 1944, Bomber Command had lost 1,100 four engine aircraft and 8,000 highly trained air crew. These numbers equate to the total destruction of 60 front line heavy bomber squadrons.

Thirty years later Jeff Gray wrote the following summary of the Battle of Berlin for Martin Middlebrook's classic book The Nuremberg Raid.

> **"I sense both then and now that our masters were disappointed in us. Berlin was a crucial battle ground for Bomber Command Command failed to achieve what the Air Marshals had set their hearts on and promised to deliver, the total destruction of the capital city and with it the will of the German nation to continue the war. It was a double failure. The city was not destroyed, nor the German will. Far from it. It was the weapon itself, our Bomber Command, that was blunted and brought close to destruction".**

At the end of his tour of operations, Jeff Gray was awarded the DFM (Distinguished Flying Medal).

Lancaster JB129 QR-G George at a Skellingthorpe dispersal October 1943

Jeff Gray's crew L-R: Paddy Morrison (MUG) Ron Jones (B/A) Jock Hay (RG) Geoff Ward (N) John McCulloch (F/E) Norman Jackson (W/Op) Jeff Gray (P)

Lofty and his ground crew mates servicing the engines on QR-G George

Flight Commander S/L Ian Fadden and crew - Skellingthorpe March 1945
L-R: W.A. Martin (N) G.G. Donald (RG) S.H. Neil (MUG) I.G. Fadden (P) H.W. Knight (B/A) S.H. Brown (W/Op) J.W. Jones (F/E)

CHAPTER 8

THE BIG CITY

Sgt E.A. Eddie Davidson DFM

Berlin raid 24th-25th March 1944: At precisely 19.09 hours our skipper, P/O Tommy Farmiloe revved Lancaster ME596 QR-H Hells-A-Poppin's powerful Merlin engines at the end of the main runway, released the brakes and shortly afterwards took off from RAF Coningsby into a dark, but clear starlit sky. After clearing the airfield circuit we settled down in our crew positions and then turned north-east over the small fishing port of Boston to join the bomber stream over the North Sea on the first outward leg of the route to Berlin.

This was our seventh trip to the Big City and the third time we had flown the favoured northerly route over Denmark. The return route back to base however was potentially a dangerous one. First of all over the north German plain, south of Hannover, then squeeze between flak batteries to the north of the dreaded Happy Valley (the Ruhr).

With 800 other main force aircraft we headed north-east over the North Sea. Two hours later we crossed the coast of Denmark just north of the island of Sylt, only a couple of miles off track, thanks mainly to the skill of our experienced second tour navigator, P/O Stan Halliwell. At the crew briefing we had been told to expect strong north-westerly winds up to 60 miles an hour at 20,000 feet. The reality was nearer 125 mph when we made our turn south east for Berlin and yet I was still getting a lower wind velocity forecast from Group. It was a ludicrous situation. Due to the high tail wind we were at our final turning point over the Baltic sea south of Denmark early and found ourselves in the first wave of the bomber stream. Apart from that everything seemed to be going very well.

As we approached the German coast between Lübeck and Rostock, bomb aimer Ken Vowe reported heavy flak and searchlights ahead. Shortly afterwards the gunners reported a burst of air to air tracer very close on the port side and shortly afterwards saw an aircraft explode and fall away in a number of burning fireballs. It was always a sickening sight to see one of our own aircraft go down. Soon afterwards the visual Monica equipment pinpointed an enemy night fighter only 500 feet away at 2 o'clock. Both gunners shouted almost together over the intercom "I can see the bastard" followed by Ray Noble, the rear gunner shouting over the intercom "Dive to port skipper". All six Brownings of the rear and mid-upper turrets started firing as the skipper dived at the start of the corkscrew manoeuvre which was so sharp and steep that after hitting my head on the roof, I ended up on the floor with all my signals books scattered around me. My stomach was in my mouth as the corkscrew seemed to go on for ever, then the skipper pulled sharply out of the dive and flew straight and level while the gunners scanned the sky. It had worked, the enemy fighter had lost us.

After getting a new course from the navigator Stan Halliwell, the skipper started to climb, hoping to get back to 20,000 feet. After picking up and sorting out my papers I realised it was time to listen out for the half hourly Met Report from Group, which again gave no indication of the true wind velocity.

About half an hour later I saw another blip on the Monica screen indicating an aircraft about 600 yards away at 11 o'clock and as I opened my mouth to yell a warning, Ray in the rear turret shouted "Enemy at 11 o'clock, corkscrew starboard go". This time I stayed in my seat having fastened my belt and heard the gunners opening up but I could still see the blip on the Monica screen following us down on the port side and I instructed the skipper "Corkscrew port". We could feel the kite shudder as the skipper tried to level out and Jerry, the flight engineer screamed, "For Christ sake Tommy, take it easy or you will tear the bloody wings off".

The violent corkscrew manoeuvre worked for we lost the fighter and as we tried to gain height Ken the bomb aimer said "I can see a glow right in front of us, it must be Berlin". Sure enough, as climbed we could see the glow spreading and there was a sigh of relief when the skipper said "We're early but I'm going in". The high winds had scattered the main force and some aircraft bombed Berlin half an hour before the Pathfinders marked the target area. It was time to listen out again for the half hourly reports from Group. With all the excitement I had missed the last two reports, so as usual I disconnected myself from the intercom and listened out on the W/T for the wind speed broadcast. Reading the message I could see they still were not reporting the actual wind speeds!

Switching the set off I suddenly became aware of a high pitched whine coming from one of the engines. In a panic, I switched back into the intercom system and heard the flight engineer saying the revs on the port inner had increased to 3,800 rpm and the skipper telling him to shut down the engine and feather the prop. This he tried to do but without success. A few minutes later I was standing in the Astrodome on fighter watch, when flames started to pour out of the faulty engine and thick smoke trailed back over the wing and tail. The skipper and engineer took emergency action to extinguish the fire by diving and side-slipping the aircraft, all to no avail. We were ordered to prepare to abandon aircraft. This was shortly followed by the flight engineer reported another engine problem. This time the revs and temperature of the port outer engine started to rise. Fearing another fire, the skipper ordered the engineer to shut down the engine immediately, which he did and successfully and feathered the prop. With both port engines dead we were in a desperate situation. The port inner was still burning with its unfeathered prop wind-milling, thereby making the aircraft very difficult to control even with full rudder trim and full opposite rudder.

By now we were approaching the illuminated target area and still on course for the aiming point. Shouting over the whine from the port inner the skipper ordered "Stand by, lets go in and drop the load and get out of the target area as quickly as possible, then we will bale out". Without a word Ken Vowe the bomb aimer got back into his position in the nose of the aircraft.

Ahead, red and green target indicators could be seen going down punctually at 22.30 hours and in the glow of the following bomb flashes on the ground and enemy searchlights I could see hundreds of black flak clouds exploding against the illuminated background. This indicated only too clearly the fierce flak barrage put up by the defenders against our attacking aircraft. With all these distractions going on around him I could hardly believe I was hearing Ken's seemingly unconcerned, quiet but distinctive Yorkshire accent begin his patter to the skipper "Left, left, no right, left again, steady!".

In the meantime molten metal and flames still poured out of the port inner engine and incredibly, the enemy's searchlights, fighters and flak batteries ignored us. Still losing height we continued our bombing run and at 22.35 hours, with a green target indicator in the bomb sight, Ken dropped our bomb load on the burning city below.

Not waiting for a target point photograph to be taken, the skipper quickly closed the bomb bay doors and turned away onto a westerly course of 208° which led to position E on the return route. Then started the debate over the intercom, should we bale out so close to the target area or try to get as far away as possible. Of course we really had no choice, if Tommy ordered us to "Bale out" we would have to go. I for one did not fancy baling out and was delighted when he decided to keep going as far as possible.

We were now down to 13,000 feet and by keeping the aircraft's indicated air speed (IAS) at 140 mph, just above stalling speed, the skipper found the fire and whine of the port inner was at a minimum but the physical effort of controlling the aircraft was taking its toll on him. At this point, Ken came out of the bomb aimers position and wrapped his arms round the rudder bars and braced himself, thus taking some of the strain off the skipper's legs. In the meantime the flight engineer tried to trim the aircraft by draining petrol from the port tanks into the two starboard wing tanks.

Despite everyone's efforts we continued losing height and at 9,000 feet we decided to jettison as much equipment as possible. Opening the starboard rear door I started by chucking out the flame floats, rest bed and even the Elsan toilet.

As I passed the D.C. power accumulator I glanced at the dial and saw it was indicating zero. Not believing it I tested my radio receiver. It was almost dead and even the interference mush was faint. I called the skipper to tell him the bad news that our electrical power was almost gone and I couldn't use the wireless transmitter. Only the generator on the starboard inner engine was working, the port inner one, because of the fire, was dead. We decided to switch off everything electrical apart from essential equipment so that with luck we might build up enough power in the accumulator to send out an SOS.

The two gunners were ordered to leave their turrets, if they tried to rotate them the accumulators would be completely drained. After much argument they agreed to dismantle their guns and with my help the six Brownings were thrown out along with all the ammunition. This left us feeling naked and defenceless. Unbelievably we had not been attacked by night fighters or been caught by flak and searchlights. We had the feeling that "somebody was looking after us". The navigation Gee box, identification friend or foe set (IFF), oxygen bottles and anything else I could lay my hands on was thrown out. The mid-upper and rear gunner, with nothing else to do, sat near me with their backs against the main spar and learned the secret of the wireless operators crew position in Lancaster aircraft. Being near the main hot air duct it was the warmest place on board.

With the Gee box gone and the radio direction finding (RDF) compass unserviceable the bomb aimer obtained a visual fix of a river east of the Zuider-Zee and a course alteration was made. In order to confirm this position the skipper asked me if I could try to get a radio fix. Switching on, I tuned to the emergency frequency and sent out an SOS. At 01.20 hours I logged a third class fix and a request for details, in code, of our situation. Nine minutes later I was given a first class fix and a further request by Group Air Traffic Control, for information. Halfway through my reply the power went, but this fix showed we were heading south down the Belgium coast.

We were now down to 4,000 feet and still losing height so the skipper decided to set a westerly course for the Norfolk coast and ordered the crew to prepare for ditching. Donning our life jackets we prayed we would not have to ditch in the cold North Sea and after what seemed like an eternity we crossed the English coast near Cromer at about 500 feet. The skipper then used his VHF R/T set to send out a Mayday call and received the reply "Give details". In the circumstances, Tommy's reply was quite polite "Just look up and you will see the problem for yourself. We are on fire". There was a pause and then a voice said "Follow the searchlights" and immediately on our port side a searchlight came on making an O on the clouds and then came down to lay a beam along the ground. As we reached the end of its light, another came on and pointed us forward. This happened three times until the runway lights of an airfield came on and we were told "Circle at 400 feet". The skipper replied "For God's sake I am at 150 feet now. I'm coming straight in".

In preparation for a possible crash landing the navigator joined the two gunners and myself as we sat facing the rear with our backs against the main spar. Ken, the bomb aimer, refused to leave his position holding the rudder bars and the flight engineer also refused to move. They both very bravely stayed to help the skipper land the aircraft. The undercarriage was then lowered but nobody knew if it was locked and would stay down or even whether the brakes would work. With tremendous effort the skipper got us down in one piece in spite of the runway lights being switched off half way down the landing run. Unfortunately, before he was able to stop the aircraft we ran out of runway and went through the boundary hedge at the end of the runway. The port inner engine fire at last went out and it was only when we climbed out on to the fuselage we saw the nose of the aircraft was embedded in a water filled ditch. "Just my luck" said Tommy "to fall off here and drown in some rotten ditch". Someone quickly answered "Not you skipper, you could walk on water tonight".

As we waited by the side of the aircraft we were puzzled why no fire engine or any other emergency vehicle had followed us to investigate our predicament. So I climbed back into the aircraft through the cockpit escape hatch to get the Very pistol and cartridges. After climbing out again I stood on the wing and started firing off some red distress flares. It was the first time I had ever had the opportunity to use the Very pistol and I enjoyed it.

About half an hour later a wagon drove up and we were taken to flying control where we found out we had landed at RAF Little Snoring, a Mosquito base near Fakenham. Later the skipper and navigator were driven away to the officers' mess while the rest of us were taken to a very cold and empty dormitory hut for what was left of the night.

In the morning after inspecting the damage to Hells-A-Poppin we waited for our Squadron to send an aircraft over to collect us. Shortly after lunch QR-O Orange arrived and we returned to base at RAF Coningsby.

Later we learned that the exceptionally strong winds experienced during the operation had scattered the main force and many aircraft flew south of the intended return route over the strongly defended Ruhr area with disastrous results. While considerable damage was inflicted on the German capital, the cost paid by Bomber Command was high with 72 aircraft failing to return. The heavies of Bomber Command were destined never to return to the dreaded Big City.

For their devotion to duty during this operation, the following RAF flying awards were made to some of the aircrew of Lancaster ME596 QR-H:
P/O H H Farmiloe (Pilot) Immediate Distinguished Service Order
F/O S Halliwell (Navigator) Distinguished Flying Cross
F/S K Vowe (Bomb Aimer) Distinguished Flying Medal
Sgt E.A.Davidson (Wireless Operator) Distinguished Flying Medal

Lancaster DV397 QR-W was lost on 24th March 1944 Berlin raid

CHAPTER 9

BOMB AIMER'S VIEW

F/S Edgar Ray

After passing the RAF aircrew selection board, I was called up in 1942 and trained as an Observer in South Africa, under the Empire Air Training Scheme, and graduated with the Winged O brevet. However, when I crewed-up at No.29 O.T.U. RAF Buntingthorpe, in 1944, there was a desperate shortage of bomb aimers. So it was from behind the bomb sight of a four-engine Lancaster that I did my tour of 30 ops with No.61 Squadron at RAF Skellingthorpe between 19th June and 27th September 1944.

On 4th July 1944, ops were on and we took off in Lancaster R5856 QR-Q on our fifth operation. The target was St.Leu d'Esserent the aiming point was a limestone hill side overlooking the river Oise. It consisted of an area of large caves tunnelled out some years before the war and used by the French to grow mushrooms. The Germans cleaned up the inside of the caves and used them to store V1 flying bombs. The aim of the attack was to collapse the roof of the caves which had been estimated to be about 25 feet thick. A subsidiary aim of the raid was to devastate the road and rail communications running between the caves and the river. At the briefing we were warned that the area was heavily defended by flak units and to keep a sharp lookout for night fighters.

This was an all 5 Group bombing operation with a few 8 Group Pathfinders. No.9 and 617 Squadrons carried the big 12,000 lb Tallboy bombs while the rest of the Lancaster force carrying about the same weight of bombs made up of 1000 lb and 500 lb HEs. Many of the bombs were fitted with six hour delay pistols. We made our attack at 01.30 hours from 15,000 feet. Throughout the bomb run the German defences threw up heavy flak and after "Bombs gone" we thankfully turned away from the target area. Suddenly, Carson Jack Foy, our rear gunner, yelled out over the intercom "Fighter Fighter corkscrew port. Go!". Skipper Harry Watkins dived the aircraft to port at the start of the corkscrew manoeuvre. At the same time we heard Jack's guns chattering away as the fighter dived past and disappeared underneath us. Shortly afterwards came a second attack and Jack called "Corkscrew" and hammered away again with his guns at the incoming fighter. This happened twice more during the next 10 minutes and Jack continued firing hundreds of rounds even though three of his four guns overheated and went and out of action.

Our extensive fighter evasion tactics had taken us gradually South of the target area and, after the final attack, north-west. This threw us off our planned course and even from my bomb aimers position I could see nothing of the ground to help with a visual fix. Eventually our navigator Doug Hockin got a good Gee fix, despite the jamming from a German radio station situated on the Eiffel Tower, and a course was set for home. We landed back at Skellingthorpe at about 03.30 hours, extremely tired after such a stressful experience. At the debrief Jack Foy reckoned that he hit the night fighter that attacked us and saw it falling away after its fourth attack. He was credited with a probable night fighter victory in his log. Anyway, we were all thankful that Jack had such good night-vision. He saved our lives that night.

The next morning our Flight armourer inspected all the aircraft's guns. He reported that the rear turret gun barrels were so worn, due to the overheating, that they must be replaced before the next sortie.

Over the following three weeks we flew another four bombing sorties against various targets in support of the Allied ground forces in France.

The sequence of events on a typical ops day at RAF Skellingthorpe was as follows.

The station tannoy would call up crews, and inform them of meal and op briefing times. Usually we ate the bacon and egg flying meal before the operation, then bomb aimers and wireless operators left for specialist briefings. Bomb aimers went to the Bombing Office that was situated at one end of a small Nissen hut. Our Bombing Leader was a second tour Aussie F/Lt Pop Nugent. The other half of the Nissen hut was the domain of No.61 Squadron's Maps and Charts Queen. A luscious, very well formed WAAF Corporal, who ensured that we all had full topographical map cover for the Continental part of our sortie.

In the Bombing Briefing we would be given details of the bomb load to be carried, total weight, bomb types, bomb delay times, position of bomb types in the bomb bay and pressure settings for the MK XIV bomb sight. All this information was recorded on the bomb aimers flight gen sheet. After the specialist briefings the crews met up in the main briefing room. As we entered this large Nissen hut, eyes were immediately drawn to a huge map of western Europe, at the far end of the building, with coloured tapes stretching across its surface indicating the route from base to target and back. Some idea of the target was deduced earlier by the crews from the amount fuel and type of bombs that had been loaded aboard the aircraft.

After the main briefing we all went to the locker room and emptied our pockets of any items that could be helpful to the enemy in the event of being shot down and captured. Next I changed into my flying kit and tested my flying helmet and oxygen mask on a test rig, drew parachute, Mae West and escape equipment. This contained a silk handkerchief map and currency of the area over which we would fly. For long night operations over Germany the gunners and bomb aimer had to wear plenty of clothing to keep warm. The heating never seemed to work properly at these crew stations resulting in sub-zero temperatures. W/Op and navigator wore minimum flying clothing because their station received blasts of excessively hot air. Only the pilot and engineer were lucky enough to work in a moderate temperature zone within the aircraft.

After kitting up, all the crews went out to the waiting buses or made their way to the aircraft dispersal on motorcycles, bikes or in their own cars.

Upon arrival at the dispersal I would first check the bomb load and sign a receipt for the bombs. We would enter the aircraft, run up engines, check all essential equipment then shut down. The skipper would then sign the Form 700 signifying that he was satisfied with the serviceability of the aircraft. We then had a tense period of waiting at the dispersal, chatting with ground crew until engine start-up time.

The dispersal was usually littered with 500 lb and 1000 lb general purpose bombs. These were left around the area as there was insufficient time to take bomb deliveries to the bomb dump where they should have been fused. The armourers usually prepared the 500 and 1000 pounders at the dispersals. Specialist bombs like the 4000 lb Cookies and 4 lb incendiaries were stored at the bomb dump. When these were required for an operation they were loaded onto bomb trolleys and driven to a fusing shed before being taken to the aircraft dispersals. When ops were on the station armourers had the dangerous and backbreaking task of bombing up each of the 40 aircraft with 5 tons of bombs. Sometimes if the target was changed it meant removing all the bombs from every aircraft and replacing them with a different type of load before de-fusing and making safe the downloaded bombs at the dispersals.

As engine start-up time approached we would board the aircraft and settle down in our take-off crew positions. Once the engines had been started we soon merged with a line of slow moving aircraft around the perimeter track and joined the queue of Lancs awaiting their turn to move forward onto the main runway for take-off. The green go light had been received from the air traffic caravan, the skipper quickly got the aircraft lumbering down the runway and off on the first leg of the route to the target area. One feature of take-off with full fuel tanks was the cones of fuel vapour which surrounded each prop and trailed well behind each wing. All very pretty but most disconcerting for the mid-upper gunner!!

When airborne, I would crawl past flight engineer Fred Jowitt through the hole into the bomb aimer's compartment in the nose of the aircraft. This area was very restricted due to the bulky packages of Window stacked inside. The bomb aimer's contribution on the way out to the target varied greatly between night and day sorties. At night, very little could be seen. On the long haul across the North Sea to targets in north Germany all was dark on reaching the enemy coastline. Getting a pin-point visual fix on the enemy coast was a hit and miss affair, resulting in many complaints from the navigator in his curtained-off office.

Flying on ops, was not all activity by any means. On many of the deep penetration sorties, long periods of anxious quiet were experienced, with George the automatic pilot engaged. Sometimes lights would be seen on the ground or stars would be reflected on the bomb aimer's clear vision panel and as these appeared to move with the oscillations of the aircraft, it was tempting to interpret them as engine exhaust flames from a night fighter. From the bomb aimer's position in the nose of the aircraft I had a 180° view of all the enemy activity en route. Despite the bomber stream being carefully routed between the known heavy flak defences, there was often someone off track flying over these areas. This soon brought a searchlight and flak reaction from below, resulting in the sight of aircraft falling away on fire and leaving burning wrecks on the ground to became a route guide to the rest of the main force.

During most of this time the bomb aimer had little to do apart from keeping a sharp lookout for other aircraft and stuffing out bundles of Window at the correct time and place to confuse the ground radar controlling the night fighters and predicted flak batteries.

The Lancaster crew's biggest blind spot was directly below the aircraft. To combat this a small perspex bubble was installed in the nose compartment. This bubble had an open rear end and was just large enough to accommodate the bomb aimer's head. By contortioning himself the bomb aimer could scan the area beneath the aircraft to check against night fighters with upward firing 20 mm cannon.

Sometimes the German fighter defences would detect the bomber stream early and release strings of parachute flares in a corridor approaching the target. Fighters would then sit up above waiting for a likely target to attack. The worst conditions were when searchlights illuminated a cloud sheet below the attacking force. This gave a perfect backdrop for high flying night fighters as dozens of bombers were silhouetted against the cloud.

On one raid our skipper, Harry Watkins, remarked that it was a particularly spectacular display and for once Doug Hockin, the navigator, got out of his seat, put his light off and poked his head out from behind his black-out curtain. He took one look and disappeared back into his chair muttering "Never again".

Half an hour from the target ETA, the wireless operator switched on the very high frequency (VHF) radio and we listened out for any instructions from the raid's Master Bomber. Nearing a target area things hotted up. Pathfinder marker flares and red and green target indicators (TIs) would be seen ahead. As the target was approached I would select the appropriate switches on the bombing panel, wind up the Mickey Mouse release timer, ensure that the aiming point photo camera (and its heater cloak) was switched on. I rechecked the MK XIV bombsight computer settings and looked out over the target area for the correct TI display. The bombing run was the time when crews were most vulnerable to defensive predicted flak batteries. Weaving was out as far as we were concerned. Not only did weaving increase the risk of collision, it also took longer to pass across the target area than flying straight and level. When the correct TIs were identified the skipper would lower his seat and flew on instruments as this gave a much steadier bombing platform. As we approached the aiming point I gave him the following instructions and he would take immediate action while repeating the instruction over the intercom.

"Bomb doors open"

"Master Switch On" (pilot operated switch for bomb release)

"Bombs Fused and Selected"

"Left, left, right, steady"

When the aiming point came into the cross wires (actually cross lights) on the sighting head, the bomb release tit was pressed and the aircraft wobbled as bombs fell off in sequence

"Bombs Gone"

"Photo Taken" (lights flashed after timed run)

"Bomb Doors closed"

"Lets get the hell out of here!"

After clearing the target area and turning onto our return course, things became quieter and I would check the bomb bay for hang ups. This was done by shining the Aldis lamp through a small door in the bomb aimer's compartment into the bomb bay. Hang ups occurred because the suspension loops on the top of some of the bombs were so roughly made that the bombs did not readily slip from the bomb cradle hooks in the bomb bay. If there were any, releasing the bomb was a fiddling task. I had to use a long hooked piece of wire to manually operate the release catch on the offending bomb station through small access panels on the aircraft floor.

After the intense activity around the target area, the long drag home seemed to go on for ever. While the tension was lower, we still had to remain vigilant all the way back home. On two occasions when nearing our base at Skellingthorpe we received the warning code word BOGRAT over the R/T. This meant that German intruders were suspected around our base area. The Bograt procedure for aircraft from each base was to fly on a designated heading, usually north-westwards until recalled for landing.

The air traffic control procedures for landing the returning bombers from operations was very slick at Skellingthorpe. Typically, one aircraft would be turning off at the far end of the runway, a second turning off halfway down, a third just gliding over the runway threshold while a fourth would be on final approach.

Daylight raids were a totally different experience for the bomber crews, and bomb aimers in particular. I could see everything that was happening ahead. The topographical maps were used continuously and map reading occupied most of my time.

Most of the daylight raids were on targets in France and after crossing the French coast I could track visually all the way to the target area. During August 1944 we took part in a few precision raids on German trench positions, troop concentrations and heavy gun emplacements. From my bomb aimer's position I saw the overall picture and dictated our aircraft's attack. These raids, only a short distance into France, were the easy ones. Sometimes however, the daylight raids were far more scary to the crew than the night sorties because one could see just how close the hundreds of other aircraft were and how thick the flak puffs were. When flying through these black smoke clouds they smelled of cordite. On 25th July 1944 our names appeared once again on the Battle Order sheet in the Squadron office. This time we were briefed to take part in a No.5 Group daylight raid against St.Cyr airfield and GAF Signals Depot (Philips factory) on the southern outskirts of Paris.

After taking off in Lancaster LM481 QR-O Orange from Skellingthorpe's main runway at 17.30 hours we soon joined up with other Lancasters to form a loose gaggle of 97 aircraft flying over the English Channel before heading inland for the Paris area. The weather was fine with continuous cloud cover at 12,000 feet and once in the target area the raid soon developed into a very concentrated attack with aircraft jockeying for position on their bombing run. At 19.55 hours we, in QR-O, commenced our run up to the target aiming point through a barrage of moderate flak. From my position in the nose of the aircraft I could see many Lancasters flying close by releasing their deadly cargo. Moments later I had the target in my bomb sight and pressed the tit to release our load of 11,450 lb HEs. Within seconds disaster struck as I felt our aircraft shudder and then fall away to starboard in an uncontrolled dive. The skipper hauled back on the control column and managed to regain control before calling over the aircraft's intercom for a damage report from all crew positions.

Ken Johnson our mid-upper gunner reported that we had been bombed from above and that a large section of the starboard wing tip was missing. Further investigation revealed that a second bomb had broken off the starboard tail-fin and rudder, while a third, had removed the whole of the rear turret carrying away Jack Foy, our rear gunner.

While the skipper fought to control our severely damaged aircraft, Johnny Ware, the W/O reported our predicament and 5 Group Flying Control diverted us to RAF Wickenby, eight miles north-east of Lincoln, for an emergency landing. Fortunately we managed to get down without any further mishap. This was our 10th operation and the loss of Jack under such circumstances was a big shock to all of us. From that day on I began to wonder if the rest of us would finish our tour in one piece.

Because of the intense operational flying schedule we had little chance of getting to know anyone else on the Squadron, apart from a working relationship with our ground crew. The sergeant in charge of our replacement aircraft, Sgt.Dixie Dean had continuously serviced an aircraft with the code QR-X X-ray since 1939 when the Squadron flew twin-engine Hampden bombers.

The ground crew had great pride in their aircraft and worked long hours to keep it serviceable for operations. We were privileged to fly their aeroplane and woe-be-tide anyone in the aircrew who left a dirty aircraft after returning from operations. Flak damage, blood, etc, were acceptable, but sandwich papers, Window wrappings and any other piece of rubbish left in the aircraft soon brought down the wrath of the ACH/Airframes on the guilty party, no matter what his rank. This aircraft, Lancaster LL911 served us well for the rest of our tour but was eventually lost on 8th-9th February 1945 while carrying out its 99th operation with the Squadron.

The cinema fiction of "Let's have a party tonight boys" just didn't exist during my period with the Squadron. An occasional night out with the crew in Lincoln, Newark or Nottingham was all we could manage, even then we ran the risk of being awakened, half sober at 03.00 hours for a dawn take-off. If flying was scrubbed for the whole of No.5 Group, then the two coach train that ran between Lincoln and Nottingham would be already overflowing with Australians from RAF Waddington, and other types, before it reached our local station at the small village of North Hykeham. The return journey was usually aboard the early morning milk train with the last few miles from Lincoln railway station to camp being on foot.

Skellingthorpe was a typical primitive wartime RAF station. The Nissen hut accommodation was abysmal. When it rained, water flowed in through the door at one end of the hut and out by the door at the other end. Our flight engineer, Fred Jowitt, would blame the puddles on his fictitious horse which he kept in the hut. Needless to say, the horse received many heavy beatings for the mess. However, we were lucky to have been able to complete our tour of operations before the winter months set in.

Like most wartime stations, Skelly was a little short of comfort in the type of accommodation on offer. The beds were iron framed and seemed minuscule to anyone who wasn't a midget. We didn't have any lockers, only one shelf and two hooks for all our belongings and washing in cold water was the norm in the ablutions.

At the end of my tour, I was commissioned and moved across the road into the Officers' Nissen huts. These were exactly the same as the N.C.Os but only had eight beds instead of fourteen. We did have an occasional Batwoman come in and clean the floor and tidy the beds. Most newly commissioned personnel found getting kitted-out with an officers No.1 uniform a protracted affair. One could buy an officer's forage cap and a Pilot Officer rank shoulder braid for your battle-dress very quickly, so this is what we wore around the station and in the officers' mess while we waiting for our new No.1 uniforms to appear. However, when going off station during this waiting period, I would wear my trusted flight sergeant kit, and eat in the Sergeants' mess before leaving camp for a night out with the boys.

Pilot Officer C.J.Foy is buried in a well cared for military grave in the centre of the local cemetery in Fontenay-le-Fleary, Versailles, France. R.I.P.

The following is a transcript of the letter written by our skipper F/O Harold Watkins to Carson 'Jack' Foy's parents in Canada.

F/O H Watkins
Officers' Mess
Royal Air Force Station,
Skellingthorpe,
Lincoln

To Jack's Parents
Dear Mr & Mrs Foy

I know that no letter of condolence from me or anyone can do much to lessen the grief caused by our tragic loss. Nevertheless I just had to tell you in what high esteem he was held by the crew and other members of the Squadron. He was a "grand lad" and I as his skipper had never found him wanting in courage and the high principles for which we are striving. I know that he saved our lives and the aircraft on more than one occasion by his fine work and these are poor words and this is poor comfort I know.

It is a terribly high price we are having to pay and I have lost many close friends. I only hope to God that when peace does come the ideals, the way of life that we're fighting for, will become a lasting reality.

Only this could justify the sacrifices that are being made today. I can't say more.

Yours very sincerely
Harold Watkins

Lancaster LL911 QR-X with F/O Harry Watkins crew in August 1944
L-R rear: Doug Hockin (N) Fred Jowitt (F/E) Johnny Ware (W/Op) Edgar Ray (B/A) Front: Harry Watkins (P) Ken Johnson (MUG) Hugh Green (RG)

Watkins crew with Lancaster centenarian ED860 QR-N Nan - August 1944

CHAPTER 10

RADIO COMMUNICATIONS

F/S A.E.Bill Perry

In November 1944 at RAF Skellingthorpe a typical ops day started at about 9 o'clock in the morning with a very informal aircrew parade to determine the number of No.61 Squadron crews available for the next operation.

After this we made our way to our aircraft's dispersal pan and checked with the ground crew that QR-X X-ray was in working order. If no air test was required we would return back to the Squadron office to check on the notice board for the latest gen on the forthcoming operation. At Skellingthorpe there was a big backboard on an easel which would carry a terse message such as:

War Tonite - Briefing 1430 - Arter yer Arters.

Our time was our own to try to relax until all the crews crowded into the mess and demolished the flying meal of bacon and eggs.

Briefing was in two parts, specialist briefings in navigation, bombing and signals. These were followed by the main briefing where we were given all the details of where we were going and why. We were told what to expect in the way of weather and defences and what action to take if we hit trouble. On attacks near the Russian lines we were actually advised to bale out over German held territory if possible, it seems the Russian troops were liable to shoot anyone not wearing a Russian uniform. In the specialist wireless operators briefing we were issued with a copy of the Bomber Code for that day. R/T (Voice) and W/T (Morse) call signs and frequencies for the stations we would be working, plus the colours of the day for the time periods covered. These codes were secret and changed every 24 hours. Some of this information had to be written on rice paper which had to be eaten by the wireless operator if an emergency arose while flying over enemy territory. After this we would visit the locker room to pick up flying clothing, parachute, emergency rations, maps and money relevant to the area we would be flying over. Thus equipped we would then be transported by crew bus to the relevant dispersals.

Once there the aircraft and all equipment would be checked over again and the ground crew would attend to anything we were not happy with, after this we would wait around until the appointed time to start engines and taxi onto the perimeter track.

This was a time of suspense because in a lot of cases the decision to go was not taken until the final minutes, depending on weather and intelligence reports etc. A white Very light fired from the control tower would indicate that the op was in doubt and if this was followed a short while later by another, it meant that the operation had been scrubbed. This was soon followed, to our everlasting shame, a loud cheer that could be heard in Lincoln 6 miles away - well almost!!

If no Very lights were seen, then engines were started at the appointed time and we joined the queue of Lancs on the perimeter track until it was our turn to line up at the end of the runway for take-off.

At Skellingthorpe, No.61 Squadron approached from the south side of the main runway and No.50 Squadron from the North. The Air Traffic controller in the caravan at the end of the runway allowed aircraft to take-off alternately from each Squadron. On a maximum effort raid this could mean controlling 30 Lancasters over a 25 minute period.

While on the threshold of the runway the aircraft was held on its brakes with engines opened up until the runway was clear, then a green Aldis light from the controller would allow you to take-off. Once airborne the course was set for the first turning point, usually with the required height being gained on the first leg. For the first twenty minutes or so the wireless operator kept a listening watch on his own station transmitter. Skellingthorpe W/T call sign was MR8, then we would switch to the No.5 Group transmitter frequency and listen out for their call sign 9SY. It was extremely important to monitor Group transmissions for messages such as upper air wind speed information for the navigator or in case there was a general recall of all aircraft. In order to keep the aircraft's wireless operator fully alert for the duration of the operation, half hour time checks were transmitted by No.5 Group head quarters. These time checks were prefixed with a random number and woe betide any wireless operator who didn't have a full set of these numbers recorded in his ops air log on landing!

When the English coast was reached the trailing radio aerial was reeled out. All emergency calls, SOS etc were made on a low frequency channel (long wave) and the trailing aerial was much better suited than the fixed aerial on top of the fuselage. Once the enemy coast was reached the trailing aerial was reeled back inside.

In between the half hour 9SY broadcasts I would spend most of my time in the Astrodome helping the gunners search the sky for German night fighters or perhaps obtaining a radio bearing for the navigator to check our position. Most navigators regarded radio fixes with suspicion but they could be reasonably accurate if care was taken.

Just before reaching the target area the very high frequency (VHF) receiver was tuned to the channel being used by the raid's Master Bomber whose job it was to circle the target area instructing and encouraging the following main bomber force. Meanwhile his wireless operator duplicated the R/T messages in case of any communication equipment malfunction.

After delivering our bombs we would clear the target area and head for home still listening out on the controllers frequency. As soon as I received the general message "Operation over - go home" from the Master Bomber, I reverted to a listening watch on No.5 Group transmissions.

On the return trip, Group would send messages giving details of the general weather conditions covering cloud base, barometric pressure etc. If any airfield became clamped with fog and a diversion to another airfield was necessary they used the W/T call signs unique to the squadron concerned.

About half an hour away from base I re-tuned to RAF Skellingthorpe's transmitter frequency to listen out for local weather reports and landing instructions. It was permitted during the return trip to break radio silence if absolutely necessary.

After landing and signing off watch, the crew was taken to the debriefing room where the first priority was a large mug of coffee with the option of a generous tot of rum added. Then followed a grilling from a debriefing officer who wanted to know how the operation had gone from our point of view.

After this we made our way to the mess for the post-op meal then back to the billet for a very welcome rest.

F/O Pearce and crew L-R: John Murray (F/E) Bill Perry (W/Op) Laurence Pearce (P) R.Barker (MUG) R Pettigrew (N) Front: D Baker (B/A) R Gillanders (RG)

Lancaster RA561 QR-T with F/O Lew Yarrall crew L-R Jack Charnock (N) Tommy Allen (F/E) Lew Yarrall (P) Les Loosemore (MUG) Bill Jenkinson (RG) Kneeling: Frank Robinson (W/Op) Charles Eldred (B/A)

CHAPTER 11

SEVEN FOR THE GOLDFISH CLUB

Max Chivers was just 19 years old when he joined the RAF in 1940. After basic training his first posting was to RAF Rochford near Southend. While on ground duties at this fighter station, he applied for aircrew duty and was accepted for pilot training. In November 1941 he crossed the Atlantic to the USA and was taught to fly at the No.2 Basic Flying Training School in California. After graduating as a pilot from the basic flying course he returned to the UK and flew twin-engine Wellingtons at an Operational Training Unit (OTU) where he crewed up with a navigator, bomb aimer, wireless operator and rear gunner. Later, in January 1943 at a Lancaster Heavy Conversion Unit (HCU) a flight engineer and mid-upper gunner was added to his crew.

After intensive crew training and accumulating the necessary number of flying hours on Lancasters, the Chivers crew was posted to No.61 heavy bomber Squadron based at RAF Syerston in Nottinghamshire.

By the start of April 1943, the crew had successfully completed ten bombing operations by attacking various industrial targets in Germany and U-boat base installations in France. On 13th April, Bomber Command heavy squadrons were briefed to attack the dock area and the naval ships in the harbour at La Spezia in Italy. This operation was regarded as a maximum range target and therefore the balance between fuel and bomb load was critical if the crews were to return safely to England.

The Chivers crew took off in Lancaster ED717 QR-S at dusk from RAF Syerston and headed south on the first leg of the 900 mile long trip over France to the target on the north-east coast of Italy.

Shortly after flying over the enemy coast of France at 20,000 feet, QR-S was attacked by two German night fighters. Both gunners opened fire on the attackers and with defensive instructions from the rear gunner, Chivers was able to lose the enemy fighters by diving the aircraft in a wild corkscrew manoeuvre. As soon as he had the aircraft under control and climbing again, Chivers called over the intercom for a new course from his navigator, but received no reply. After a short interval the wireless operator, Danny Shea, reported that the navigator was unwell, and in his opinion would not be taking part in the rest of the operation. Under these circumstances Chivers could have aborted the operation and returned to base, but as they were half way to the target he decided to press on. By using his route map plus a visual fix from the bomb aimer a new course was set for La Spezia. Two hours later as the aircraft was approaching the target area, Chalky White, the mid-upper gunner reported seeing another night fighter on the starboard side and after giving it a long burst of fire from his twin Brownings, the fighter dived away and was not seen again. After five and a half eventful hours, they arrived in the target area. Most of the other 200 main force Lancasters had already blitzed the area leaving behind many large fires and a huge column of smoke rising from the docks and oil depot area. After assessing the situation from 8,000 feet Chivers turned his Lancaster onto its bombing run and ran a gauntlet of defensive fire from both harbour and naval ship flak before the bomb aimer released the bomb load. On clearing the target area over the Mediterranean, a north-westerly course was set for home. This heading took them over the Rhone valley in the south of France and then in a westerly direction to exit the enemy coast south of the Cherbourg peninsular.

Four hours after leaving the target area, the flight engineer reported a serious loss of fuel, possibly due to flak damage. Chivers realised they were in a desperate situation. They had already been in the air for almost ten hours and he was uncertain of their true position along the return route. However, he decided to carry on in the hope of reaching an airfield on the south coast of England for an emergency landing rather than abandoning the aircraft over enemy territory. An hour later, flying over the sea in a north westerly direction and almost out of fuel, F/O Chivers ordered his crew to take up their ditching positions and sent out a Mayday call, giving their approximate position.

As dawn was breaking Chivers turned the aircraft into wind before putting QR-S skilfully down on the Atlantic swell. The impact broke the aircraft's back near the mid-upper turret but it kept afloat long enough for the crew to escape.

The crew, although badly shaken were otherwise unhurt and soon clambered out of the emergency ditching exit above the aircraft's main spar and onto the port wing. After releasing the dinghy from its storage position, they all scrambled aboard with their emergency rations. Unfortunately, in his haste to get out, the navigator left the emergency portable radio inside the sinking aircraft. So began a distressing and unhappy time for all the crew. They had come down half way between Cherbourg in France and the Isles of Scilly. Without the radio they would have to wait and hope the air sea rescue organisation could find them. However, their chances of being picked up by friendly shipping in this area were slim because they were too far away from the coastal shipping lanes along the southern coast of England. Nonetheless, as the weather remained good and the sea calm, they had a good chance of surviving a long exposure to the elements.

For two days the despondent crew drifted in the small open dinghy and saw no ships or aircraft to raise their hopes of rescue. Suddenly during the morning of the third day they heard the sound of an aircraft and fired off some red distress flares. This attracted the attention of a twin-engine Whitley of Coastal Command which was returning to its base from a U-boat patrol of the Bay of Biscay. Moments later the Whitley flew low over the now elated and waving crew of QR-S. Fortunately their luck held and the weather remained good throughout the day. Late in the afternoon, much to the crew's relief, they saw a Royal Navy air sea rescue launch heading towards them.

Once aboard they were given a great reception by the sailors, several tots of rum, dry clothes and then quickly taken to the naval base on the Isles of Scilly. After recovering from their harrowing ordeal, the Chivers crew, apart from the navigator, who was suffering from operational fatigue, returned to RAF Syerston to continue their tour of operations.

Flying Officer Max Chivers was awarded the Distinguished Flying Cross for his gallantry and leadership. All of the crew of Lancaster ED717 QR-S Sugar qualified to become members of the Goldfish Club.

The Chivers crew and dinghy are taken aboard the Air Sea Rescue launch

Chivers crew aboard ASR launch. Back row L-R: E.G.Smith (RG) M James (B/A) V.A.Rimmer (N) E.Vale (F/E) Front row: S.A.White (MUG) M.Chivers (P) D.Shea (W/Op)

CHAPTER 12

OPERATION HYDRA

(Peenemünde)

Sgt Charles A.Cawthorne

Having joined the RAF as a Boy Apprentice, I volunteered for aircrew duties as a flight engineer and at the age of eighteen found myself posted from No.1660 Heavy Conversion Unit (HCU), Swinderby, along with the rest of our newly formed Lancaster crew to No.467 RAAF Squadron based at RAF Bottesford, in Leicestershire.

The Station Commander was a very experienced bomber pilot, Wing Commander L Gomm, and the Squadron Commander was Squadron Leader Green. Both men were keen to show the rest of No.5 Group what an Aussie squadron could do and to this end were keen to build one of the highest totals of operational sorties within the Group. The Squadron flew their first operational Gardening (mine laying) sorties on 2nd-3rd January 1943. These were quickly followed by an Oboe trial bombing operation against Essen in the Ruhr valley.

Our crew's first operational sortie was on 2nd April 1943 when we bombed the strongly defended U-boat pens at St Nazaire. As we approached the target Harry Crumplin, the navigator, was persuaded to come forward into the cockpit to see the target area ahead all lit up with searchlights, TIs, and the irregular flashes from exploding bombs and flak. He took one look, muttered "Bloody Hell" and quickly disappeared behind the black curtain around his crew position. In complete contrast to this experience, less than 24 hours after facing the flak of St Nazaire, I accompanied our wireless operator, David Booth, to his wedding in Manchester. Our tour of operations progressed very satisfactorily and we soon found ourselves involved in what was referred to in the newspapers as The Battle of the Rhur. Despite Bomber Command sustaining heavy casualties during this period, our crew remained relatively unscathed but nevertheless we were alarmed to find that every time we went on leave, another crew become a squadron casualty whilst using our aircraft.

By early August 1943, we had completed 24 operational sorties and our crew were known as one of the old sweats of the Squadron. Together with other experienced crews, we were taken off routine bombing trips and became engaged in special low level time and distance bombing practice over the Wainfleet bombing range near Skegness. At first we thought it strange that it was the most experienced crews who were degraded in this way but as the results were being scrutinised by senior staff from Group Headquarters, headed by the Air Officer Commanding (AOC) Air Vice Marshal Cochrane, we soon realised that there was some hidden purpose behind this special training. A few days later the AOC visited Bottisford and told the selected aircrews that they must do better and reduce the number of bombing errors. At this stage we had no idea what was going on but there were rumours circulating around the camp that we might be going to attack the German dams again or maybe the Dortmund-Ems canal.

On 17th August all speculation ended when we were detailed to attend the pre-operation briefing and it immediately became apparent that something very special had been planned. Security around the operations block was unusually severe with RAF Police in far greater numbers than usual. There was a great buzz of speculation amongst the crews as we entered the large briefing room. The assembled crews were brought to attention as the station's senior officers entered the room accompanied by a very senior officer from Group Headquarters. The curtain over the map of western Europe was pulled back to reveal red route marker tapes leading to a small target called Peenemünde on the German Baltic coast sited between Rostock and Stettin. I wondered what all the fuss was about because we had never heard of this little place called Peenemünde and the Squadron had attacked both Rostock and Stettin quite recently.

The briefing was opened with a statement from the visiting officer from Group. He said "Peenemünde is a German military research establishment whose scientists are working on new Radio Detection Finding (RDF) equipment as a countermeasure against our night bombers and therefore is a very important target that has to be destroyed at all costs. That is why the operation has been planned to take place in full moon flying conditions and must be carried out at low level. It is imperative that this target is destroyed and I must warn you that if you are unsuccessful tonight, then the Squadron will have to return tomorrow night and on successive nights until complete destruction is achieved". It was only later when the V2 rockets started to fall on London in September 1944, that we in Bomber Command and the general public learned the true purpose of this raid i.e. the destruction of the secret V2 rocket research and production facility.

The Squadron Commander then said it was to be a precision attack on three main target areas. The first and second waves would attack on Pathfinder TIs but No.5 Group squadrons were to bomb last in the third wave, and would use the new time and distance bombing method as the target would probably be obscured by smoke from the first and second wave attacks.

The objective for the third wave aircraft was the Experimental Works which consisted of over 70 small buildings. This complex contained vital development data and equipment and the accommodation block which housed the V2 Project Director, General Dornberger and his Deputy, Wernher von Braun. We did not learn this until much later. The crews were then informed that a Master Bomber, Group Captain John Searby of No.83 Pathfinder Squadron, would control all phases of the raid by circling the target area and if necessary give instructions over the VHF radio to the Pathfinders should the TIs need re-positioning or to stop main force creep-back developing. As we listened to the briefing it became clear that this operation was a formidable task but we were determined to succeed as none of us fancied our chances of survival if we had to return again the next night. At 21.30 hours our Aussie skipper, Warren Pluto Wilson, turned our heavily laden Lanc onto the main runway and once the aircraft was lined up he slowly opened the throttles while I watched the needles swing round in the boost and rev gauges. At the same time my left hand followed the skipper's right as he pushed forward the throttle levers. As the aircraft gained speed the navigator called out the indicated air speed (IAS) over the intercom. With full rudder control and all four engines pulling, the skipper called for me to take over the throttle levers and push them through the gate for maximum power. Moments later with gauges showing 3,000 rpm +14 lb/sq.in. boost, the aircraft reached a speed of 100 knots IAS and took off into a cloudless summer evening sky. With a positive rate of climb established the skipper called for the undercarriage to be raised and engines set to a climbing power of 2,850 rpm with +9 lb/sq.in.

boost. This was quickly followed by a series of flap adjustments and once the airframe was clean, our Lancaster PO-F Freddie climbed away at 155 knots to join the third wave of the bomber stream off the north Lincolnshire coast. To see scores of heavy bombers assembling in bright moonlight over the North Sea was quite an exhilarating experience. Usually we carried out ops on dark moon-less nights and the only indication other aircraft were around was when we ran through prop wash turbulence or occasionally we saw the red glow from aircraft engine exhausts.

At 23.35 hours we crossed the Danish coast twelve miles north of the island of Sylt and from our operational height of 18,000 feet I could clearly see small villages and farm houses in the brightly lit countryside. Forty minutes later we were flying over the Baltic and the moonlight presented an eerie picture as numerous islands were clearly outlined against the sea. At this juncture we were flying southeast at 8,000 feet some twenty miles off shore, midway between Rostock and Stettin. In the nose of the aircraft our Aussie bomb aimer, Swill Campbell, was busy map reading and called over the intercom that we were approaching the headland of Arkona on the north-eastern tip of the island of Rügen. We were now only 40 miles from the target and the skipper turned south to followed the coastline that led directly to Peenemünde.

Approaching the target we could see the raid ahead progressing as the first and second wave aircraft bombed the red and green TIs laid down by the Pathfinders and from our position at the rear of the bomber stream there appeared to be little enemy opposition with only moderate light flak and few searchlights. Over our VHF radio set we heard the calm voice of Group Captain Searby assuring the third wave crews the raid was progressing in a satisfactory way and to standby for further orders.

A few minutes later at 00.42 hours the Master Bomber ordered the Lancasters of 5 Group to commence their timed bombing runs from the designated starting point at the southern tip of the island.

At this point during every bombing raid, aircraft became particularly vulnerable to flak or night fighter attack and on this occasion the seven mile bombing run seemed endless as we frantically searched the crowded sky for the enemy and to avoid a collision with a friendly aircraft. At last, our bomb aimer announced "Bombs gone" and the aircraft wobbled as it was relieved of its heavy load.

The skipper held the same course until the aiming point photograph had been taken and then much to the relief of everyone on board turned back over the sea to start our journey home.

As we left the immediate target area, we felt elated that our outward flight had been uneventful and we had made a successful bombing run, but as we commenced our return journey we became aware of increased enemy activity in our vicinity as burning aircraft began to fall out of the sky at an alarming rate. It seemed as if the third wave of the bomber stream was being attacked by a huge armada of enemy night fighters who were taking full advantage of the bright moonlight conditions.

Later, we found out that the German night fighters had been successfully lured away from the Peenemünde area by a diversionary raid on Berlin. However, once the German fighter controllers realised that this was not the main target, the night fighters were ordered to pursue the bombers over Peenemünde.

The skipper called over the I/C for everyone to be extra vigilant but without warning we felt our aircraft judder as it was riddled with both machine gun and 20 mm cannon fire. Standing beside the pilot, I clearly recall seeing tracer bullet trails looping high over our port wing and hearing the terrifying noise of the enemy's ammunition hitting our aircraft. George Oliver, our mid-upper gunner, made an immediate response to the attack and our rugged Australian skipper put the aircraft into a violent dive to port in the hope of escaping further attention from the fighter. However, after losing several thousand feet of altitude he announced he was having great difficulty in getting the aircraft out of the dive. Without further ado I leaned over to assist by grasping the control column with both hands and together we pulled it back until the aircraft responded and we were flying straight and level again.

On recovery, I checked the engine gauges and fuel control panel and looking aft saw what looked like the whole of the rear fuselage on fire with thick black acrid smoke billowing forward. Out of the smoke climbing over the main spar came George the mid-upper gunner and he was soon joined by David the wireless operator. Both had their chutes clipped on ready to jump out of the front emergency exit. I reported the fire to the skipper and expected him to give the order to abandon aircraft, but to my amazement he cooly said "Well go and put the bloody thing out then". If it had not been for those cool calculated words, we would have all finished our ops tour there and then.

Armed with fire extinguishers, George and I went aft over the main spar to tackle the blaze and there we were quickly joined by David. We found the ammunition lines to the rear turret ablaze with one round setting fire to the next with alarming speed. The fuselage was full of thick smoke which made our progress difficult and soon it was realised the dead mans handle, a device for rotating the rear turret in the event of hydraulic failure, had received a direct hit. The turret's hydraulic oil supply had been sprayed around the floor not only adding fuel to the fire but making it difficult to stand in our rubber flying boots. When all extinguishers had been emptied, we resorted to smothering the blaze with our gloved hands and eventually we succeeded in putting the fire out.

It was then that we realised the rear gunner, Paddy Barry, was wounded and trapped in his turret. With the aid of the aircraft axe, George, the mid-upper gunner managed to open the back doors of the rear turret and I assisted in manoeuvring Paddy over the tailplane and up to the rest bed near the main spar. Despite Paddy's precarious state, we had to leave him and return to our crew positions to report on the fire damage sustained from the night fighter attack and take stock of the battle that was taking place all around us in the bomber stream. From the flight engineer's panel I calculated that we were losing a considerable amount of fuel and after reporting this to the skipper and navigator it was decided we would divert to an airfield in neutral Sweden. At this juncture Swill, the bomb aimer, and I were told by the skipper to make Paddy as comfortable as possible. By the light of a masked torch, we realised he had sustained a serious injury to his left foot from an exploding cannon shell. I attempted to inject morphine to ease his pain but could not get through his protective clothing. In desperation, I started to cut away his flying boot which was torn and saturated with blood. In the semi-darkness of the fuselage it was difficult to see any detail and what I thought to be a large piece of boot was in fact a piece of skin which I immediately replaced and bound the wound with a shell bandage. I then returned to my seat in the cockpit and after rechecking the fuel gauges I realised the self sealing fuel tanks had been effective and the loss of fuel had been stemmed. Following a hurried crew conference, it was decided we had sufficient fuel to attempt the return journey over the North Sea to England.

The skipper then announced he was still having trouble controlling the aircraft which continuously wanted to climb and it was necessary for him to stand on the rudder pedals and wedge his back against the seat with fully extended arms to prevent the aircraft climbing. In an endeavour to relieve the physical effort of the situation the skipper and I removed our Mae Wests and after inflating them jammed them both between the control column and the pilot's seat. We did not realise that the problem was caused by the loss of our elevator trim tabs which had been shot away during the night fighter attack.

By the time we crossed the enemy coast the skipper was completely exhausted and it became necessary for me to fly the aircraft over the relatively safe area of the North Sea. With great difficulty we changed seats and by the grace of God, nothing untoward happened during the sea crossing. Approaching the Lincolnshire coast the skipper took over again and David Booth, the wireless operator, called our base for a priority landing due to our seriously wounded gunner and the precarious state of the aircraft. Bottesford responded to our request and the skipper ordered all crew members to their crash positions for an emergency landing. I had to remain in my normal crew position to assist the skipper with the handling of the aircraft. On final approach, I was fully prepared to select full flap which was the normal procedure but the skipper quickly reminded me that only a couple of weeks before an Aussie pilot on the Squadron called Tillotson had suffered a complete fracture of the rear fuselage on his aircraft following full flap selection after suffering serious battle damage to the rear fuselage. His aircraft's tail fell off with disastrous results. I didn't require any further warning and my hand kept a respectful distance away from the flap lever.

In the early morning light after nearly seven hours in the air we glided over the threshold of the runway and touched down at 04.20 hours. With engines spluttering we taxied off the runway and came to a stop on the grass, where we were immediately attended by the fire and ambulance staff who carefully extricated Paddy, our injured gunner.

It was now quite light and on evacuating the aircraft through the rear door, I was amazed to see the extent of the damage we had sustained. Internally the skin of the rear fuselage was charred and black from the intense fire and shafts of light pointed to where machine gun bullets and cannon shells had entered and exited the aircraft. Externally, the wings, rear fuselage, tail plane and both rudders were all severely perforated by machine gun and cannon fire. Overall PO-F Freddie was in a appalling state, but miraculously all four engines were undamaged and had functioned perfectly throughout the flight to bring us home.

After debriefing, we went for our post-op egg and bacon breakfast. Before retiring to our billets for a well earned rest we visited sick quarters to see Paddy before he was transferred to the local hospital. He later became one of plastic surgeon McKindoe's wartime guinea pigs and was ultimately fully restored to health despite a much damaged ankle.

Two days later we were all delighted to hear that our skipper had gained the immediate award of the DFC and George Oliver the mid-upper gunner, who was confirmed as having shot down the attacking Me109 before vacating his turret, was awarded the Conspicuous Gallantry Medal. All the remaining crew members received the appropriate DFC or DFM decoration at the end of the tour.

Within days of this episode, we were on operations again and following two raids on Berlin our crew were awarded Tour Complete status by the Squadron Commander on 9th September 1943.

We were in fact the first crew to survive a tour of bombing operations with No.467 RAAF Squadron since it was formed at RAF Scampton in November 1942. After an end of tour leave, I was then posted with my skipper to No.1668 HCU at RAF Balderton and later carried out staff engineer duties with No.1660 HCU at RAF Swinderby. This was followed by ground instructor duties at the Lancaster Holding Unit at RAF Scampton.

The Crew of Lancaster JA675 - PO-F Freddie

Pilot	W/O Warren Wilson DFC RAAF
Flight Engineer	Sgt Charles A Cawthorne DFM RAF
Navigator	Sgt Harry Crumplin DFM RAF
Bomb Aimer	F/O Swill Campbell DFC RAAF
Wireless Operator	Sgt David Booth DFM RAF
Mid Upper Gunner	Sgt George Oliver CGM, RAF
Rear Gunner	Sgt Patrick Barry DFM RAF

L-R: Harry Crumplin, Dave Booth, Warren Wilson, Swill Campbell, Charles Crawthorne and George Oliver

Second Tour:
In July 1944 I was called back to do a second tour of operations and joined F/Lt Hugh Horsley's crew at No.1661 HCU, RAF Winthorpe near Newark. We first flew together as a crew in a Stirling on 20th July 1944.

On 2nd September we started our Lancaster training at No.5 Lancaster Finishing School, RAF Syerston, and eight days later were posted to No.61 Squadron at RAF Skellingthorpe. On posting, our skipper was promoted to Squadron Leader and immediately took command of one of No.61 Squadron Flights.

On 17th September 1944 we flew our first operational sortie against the French port of Boulogne in veteran Lancaster EE176 Mickey The Moocher QR-M. It was the aircraft's 107th operation. Little did I know that my second tour of operations with No.61 Squadron was destined to end over Holland a week later.

CHAPTER 13

LANCASTER QR-K KING IS MISSING

On 24th September 1944 a BBC radio news programme gave out brief details of the previous night's bombing operation carried out by No.5 Group. In essence the news reader announced: **"Last night RAF Lancasters of Bomber Command carried out a successful attack on the Dortmund-Ems-Canal. Fourteen of our aircraft failed to return to their bases".**

At RAF Skellingthorpe near Lincoln, preparation for this raid started early in the day when ground crews of No.50 and No.61 Squadron carried out routine maintenance and later loaded 14,000 lb of HE bombs and 1,500 gallons of fuel aboard each aircraft.

The main operational briefing for the aircrews started at 15.00 hours. They were told this was a No.5 Group Operation and the objective was to breach the banks of the Dortmund-Ems-Canal near Ladbergen, just north of Münster. The aiming point was the twin aqueducts over the river Grane where the level of the canal water is higher than the surrounding land. If the crews were successful in draining this section of canal it would halt the barge traffic for a while from carrying vital raw materials between the North Sea ports and the industrial Ruhr.

Take-off time for the thirty Skellingthorpe Lancasters was set to start at 19.00 hours and the route selected was a direct track of 350 miles on an easterly heading of 110 degrees. This took the heavy bombers over the North Sea to the Scheldt Estuary and then across Holland to the target area in northwest Germany. One of the aircraft taking part in the raid was No.61 Squadron Lancaster, LM718 QR-K King. It was a comparatively new aircraft with only 45 hours flying time in its maintenance log. Its skipper, S/L Hugh Horsley AFC, was the Squadron's A Flight commander and a very experienced pilot having recently joined the Squadron from Training Command. This was the crew's fourth operation together and after taking off at 19.17

hours they soon settled down in their crew positions on the first leg of the flight to join up with the main force of 135 Lancasters and five Mosquitos heading out over the North Sea.

By the time QR-K had reached the Dutch coast it was flying at an altitude of 20,000 feet and ahead the crew could see occasional bursts of scattered flak and searchlights lazily roving across the night sky.

Twenty minutes later in the Eindhoven area the mid-upper gunner saw a twin-engine night fighter coming in for an attack and opened fire with his twin Brownings while yelling out over the intercom "Skipper corkscrew port. Go". Horsley immediately responded to the instruction by diving the aircraft to the left while the rest of the crew hung on in the blackness to whatever they could while the aircraft gyrated in this dramatic manoeuvre. Throughout this defensive action the two gunners reported the position of the fighter. Suddenly, after the fifth corkscrew, the Messerschmitt Bf110 attacked again from the rear port quarter and opened fire with its 20 mm cannon and machine guns hitting the vulnerable Lancaster in the centre of the fuselage and port wing.

Inside QR-K the crew felt their aircraft judder from the fighter's devastating fire which left the mid-upper gunner and the wireless operator either dead or seriously wounded and a power loss on both port engines. Within seconds the Lancaster was coned by searchlights and this was quickly followed by a barrage of exploding shells from the Eindhoven flak batteries. The skipper responded to the danger by putting the aircraft into a high speed dive to escape the searchlights and deadly flak. Unbeknown to Horsley the aircraft had also sustained damage to the control system and it took all his strength to apply enough backward pressure on the control column before the aircraft responded and they were flying straight and level once again.

They were now down to 10,000 feet and after quickly weighing up the situation Horsley decided the best course of action was to abort the operation, lighten the aircraft and return to base. As navigator Jack Webber worked out a course for home, the bomb doors were opened and the bombs were quickly jettisoned over the Dutch countryside. Even after trimming the aircraft S/L Horsley still found it difficult to control and with the two port engines shut down they continued to lose altitude at an alarming rate. The situation was now grave so Horsley had no alternative, he ordered "GET OUT" and the crew abandoned the crippled aircraft.

The first one out was rear gunner Reg Hoskisson who was wearing a fighter pilots parachute so all he had to do was unplug his oxygen pipe and intercom lead before rotating his turret to the right, opened its back doors and rolled out backwards into the aircraft's slipstream.

Meanwhile up front in the nose, bomb aimer Johnny Wheeler jettisoned the escape hatch in his compartment and quickly disappeared through the gaping black hole. Flight engineer Charlie Cawthorne should have been the next man out but was having problems locating his parachute under a pile of Window packages. In his panic a number of the bundles were thrown in the direction of Jack Webber who had just left his seat and was moving towards the forward escape hatch. Moments later in the darkness of the cockpit, he pushed past Cawthorne, who was in the process of clipping on his chute, and rapidly departed through the hole in the B/A's compartment floor.

By this time Hugh Horsley had set the automatic pilot and was leaving his seat so without further delay Cawthorne pulled off his oxygen mask and helmet and dived head first through the hatch from the cockpit step and was quickly followed by his skipper.

The aftermath:

Lancaster LM718, QR-K King crashed near the village of Deurne in the southeast of Holland at approximately 22.30 hours on 23rd September 1944.

The Crew's fate:

S/L H.W.Horsley AFC	Pilot,	Evaded
P/O C.A.Cawthorne DFM	Flt/Eng	Evaded
F/O J.C.Webber	Navigator	PoW
F/O J.P.Wheeler	Bomb Aimer	PoW
F/S G.Twyneham	Wireless Op	Killed
Sgt H.W.Jennings	Air Gunner	Killed
Sgt R.T.Hoskisson	Air Gunner	Evaded

F/S Twyneham and Sgt.Jennings are both buried at the Ventry military war cemetery in the Netherlands.

The van Hout sisters on Lancaster LM718 QR-K King - 25th September 1944

CHAPTER 14

DUTCH ENCOUNTER

Sgt. Reg Hoskisson

Ten minutes after the night fighter attack and our defensive Corkscrew manoeuvres the Skipper gave the Bale-Out order over the intercom.

I was fortunate because I was wearing a fighter pilot's parachute and all I had to do was rotate the Rear Turret, disconnect my oxygen mask and intercom, pull the lever to open the rear door of the turret lean back and the aircrafts slip stream sucked me out of the turret.

The next thing I knew I was floating downward, everything was quiet and peaceful just faint hum of the wind in the shroud lines of the parachute. Looking down I noticed hundreds of small fires burning on the ground and concluded they must be the incendiary bombs and flares we had jettisoned. As I descended I could also see trees and hedges taking shape. I was not dropping straight down as I imagined but travelling over the ground at a very fast pace. At a height of about 50ft I saw my first German soldiers running across a field towards me.

I braced my legs in a forward position for the inevitable impact as one of the soldiers who had totally misjudged my speed came towards me. I hit him full in the face with my feet and his arms flew up in the air as he rolled backwards on the ground. The next thing I knew the wind had filled the canopy and I was rising again and travelling at high speed away from my pursuers. When I eventually touched down the ground was very soft and sandy, but before I could get free of my parachute another gust of wind filled the canopy and I was airborne again. Twice this happened but the third time I managed to run forward and fall on top of the canopy to prevent it becoming re-inflated.

It was at this point the gravity of my situation hit me. Here I was all on my own in enemy territory. Now what was I to do? Then suddenly all those lectures in ice cold lecture rooms came flooding back and the Flying Officer Instructors saying '*Pay attention Cadet*

Hoskisson it might happen to you. Remember the first thing you do is BURY YOUR PARACHUTE.'

Trying to gather up some 60 yards of silk in a wind blowing about 40 miles per hour was not as easy as the instructors had suggested but by lying flat out on top of it I managed to gather the chute underneath me and wrap the shroud lines round it, until it looked like a large bundle of washing.

I began to walk and eventually came to a small hedgerow and on looking round the other side I discovered a ditch about 3 ft deep overgrown with weeds, it was a good place to bury my chute, in it went and I covered it up with dead leaves so nothing could be seen. Having disposed of my chute I began to look round and found I was standing on an overgrown cart track deeply rutted with the wheels of farm carts. I began to follow this track which eventually led me to the approaches of a small farm. Again my mind went back to the lecture rooms of RAF Training command '*Be careful when approaching your first contact, make sure no Germany Army transport is parked there, check to see if the house is on the telephone while the occupant may appear to be friendly, making you coffee, some one else may be phoning up to the local German Commandant'*.

I looked around the farm buildings, no German trucks, no telephone wires, the place was well isolated, not a chink of light from any window or door. I stood for some moments listening and decided to take a chance. As I was walking towards the house looking for a door, a dog began to bark. I stood very still but the dog knew his job and barked louder than ever.

Suddenly the door opened and against the dimly lit background I could see a man standing in the doorway. Cautiously I approached the man and we looked at each other as if neither of us had ever seen a human being before. I asked him if he was Dutch, he drew himself up and said 'HOLLANDER'. I think he mistook my 'Dutch' for Deutch, and said 'Deutchland Kaput' and spat on the ground, from that moment I knew I was in safe hands.

I pointed to the sky and said RAF, he came forward and almost dragged me into the house. The next few minutes were complete confusion, he told his wife I was a 'British Tommie' I think the poor chap thought the village had been liberated. Then a little girl about 10 years old appeared 'Winston Churchill' she said and gave the 'V' sign.

The child was quick to grasp who I was and what I wanted. I produced my escape map of Holland and she pointed on the map to a place called Deurne, near Helmond quite close to the German frontier. I gathered from her that there were German troops in the area. I underlined Deurne and she took the pencil from me and in a few seconds she had marked swastikas all around the area.

The pencil was a Venus, dark green with gold markings, she looked at the pencil with eyes wide open so I said she could keep it. Later I realised this simple act of kindness could have had fatal consequences for the family.

She explained my situation to her parents and after a short discussion the girl told me her father knew someone who might be able to help me and would go to see him later. Meanwhile, his good lady produced a pot of coffee, bread, cheese and two hard boiled eggs. My contribution to this feast was a bar of chocolate from my emergency rations.

I gathered from the little girl their family name was Hooning and she was learning English and listened to the BBC broadcasts, which was strictly forbidden by the Germans.

After supper Mr Hooning put on his hat and coat and went out. While he was away doubts began to cross my mind. I really couldn't blame him if he turned me over to the Germans because after all he had a wife and child to care for and he knew the penalty for helping an Allied airman to escape was death.

About an hour later he returned accompanied by a young man with a dark complexion. He came forward with an out-stretched hand and a large grin on his face. He introduced himself in quite good English 'My name is Jo. Welcome to our country.'

In a few words I explained to him that I had baled out of an RAF aircraft after a German night-fighter attack. He listened very carefully to my story asking what our target was, what type of aircraft, and then as if checking every detail, asked me where my parachute was. I told him it was buried in a ditch along side the cart track leading to the farm. He whispered something to Mr Hooning and then asked me to go with them to find it. I suspected he was a member of the Dutch underground movement and I had to prove to him that I was a genuine British Airman and not a German plant.

We soon found the parachute and Jo seemed much relieved as we returned to the farm house kitchen. Jo asked me if I carried the usual photographs, I said 'Yes I have three, which one do you want?'

These photographs were part of an airman's escape kit. The photographs fitted exactly into Dutch, Belgium and French identification cards. Full face for France, left profile for Belgium and right profile for the Dutch.

Jo was obviously satisfied that I was an evader and began to outline his short term plans for me. He said I could only stay here one night otherwise the family would be put in great danger and the child might talk.

The plan was that I would go to church with the family tomorrow morning dressed in Mr Hooning's best suit and shoes. Jo said I had nothing to fear from the Germans as they could be fooled all the time providing you behaved naturally. After mass he would take me to a safe house where he was staying, with other members of the underground. I found out later this was the headquarters of the local underground movement.

I explained to Jo I carried Dutch currency and could pay if money was required. I produced a 200 Guilder note and asked whether I could give this to Mr Hooning for his suit and shoes.

Jo said they were a very poor family and the note was a large denomination. If they spent it in the local shop it would attract attention in such a small village. However, he decided to give the note to Mr Hooning on the understanding that on no account was he to spend it until Deurne was liberated by the allies, as he might bring misfortune on himself and his family.

After Jo left, Mrs Hooning and her daughter went to bed. Mr Hooning sat with me by the dying fire enjoying one of my Players cigarettes.

I could not sleep or even doze for thinking about the rest of the crew, had they all managed to escape or by some strange freak had the Skipper got control of the aircraft and returned to base minus his rear gunner. I idly wondered if poor old Hugh could talk his way out of that but was sure he could as he was training to be a lawyer in civilian life.

Sunday 24th September

It was now early morning, the fire had gone out and it was cold. Mrs Hooning came downstairs and quickly relit the fire with kindling and logs and then made coffee. It was made from acorns and tasted awful but least it was hot and warmed me up. She then produced slices of ham, bread and cheese and pork dripping.

I changed into Mr Hoonings best suit and although the shoes were a bit tight I managed to walk ok. My uniform and parachute were then burnt in the farmyard as nothing must be left to indicate to the Germans I had been there.

Jo arrived at 6am and told me what to expect over the next few hours. He then asked me if I had given the family anything. At first I said 'no' but then remembered the pencil I had given to the little girl the previous evening. After examining it he pointed to the markings -Venus Pencil Co Made in England. He said 'if she had taken that to school everyone would want to know how she came by it'. The girl returned the pencil with tears in her eyes. I felt awful and although Jo gave her his own pencil it did not console her.

Shortly afterwards we all walked to the church for mass. I must admit I felt very uneasy as everyone looked at me and wondered who I was. After the service Jo and I casually walked from the church with other villagers down the main street before entering a large house that stood close to the road.

I was introduced to the owner of the house and his wife although no names were mentioned. I was then introduced to another man who spoke very good English. He asked me where I lived in England and when I said Birmingham, he immediately asked me to name the two railway stations. I said 'Snow Hill and New Street'. He smiled and then wanted to know which was the best football team in Birmingham.

My reply 'West Bromwich Albion' produced a very blank look so I followed this by saying 'others would say Aston Villa but you did asked for the best team.'

He then reached in his pocket and handed me a Dutch Identification card. They had given me the name Peter Van Loom.

Jo then said, 'What is your name?' I repeated the name on the card in my Brumy accent and they all laughed at my pronunciation. Jo said 'you may fool the Germans but not the Dutch Police'.

They assured me the identity card was genuine as it had been signed by both the Dutch Burgomaster and German Commandant.

I was then told my plane had been found and two of the crew had died in the crash. They were being buried that morning by a German troop with the usual military honours. I was assured the local people would look after the graves.

The death of my comrades was a shock and I had to turn away and look through the window. The crew had been together for 12 months and we were all good friends.

As I gazed out at the window I saw German soldiers coming down the road. The men looked haggard and drawn, dirty and unshaven just slowly moving along with a fixed stare.

My new friends told me the troops were being withdrawn across the frontier as they could no longer be relied on to fight.

These troops consisted of Latvians and Poles who had joined the German Army when things were good, now they were no longer interested in the Fatherland and Hitler's New Reich. They had been without food and for the past 48 hours RAF Typhoons fighter bombers had wrecked their transports and petrol dumps.

Apparently the road all the way to Eindhoven was littered with trucks and the local people expected Deurne to be liberated by the Allies within 24 hours.

We sat down and drank more coffee and I watched the endless file of German troops pass by the window. As I watched a soldier made a dash towards a wood across a field throwing away his rifle in the ditch. The German NCO in charge raised his submachine gun and fired a short burst. The man fell without a sound and the troop kept walking, no one crossed the road to see whether he was dead or alive.

At last the road was clear of German troops and at about 10.30am four British armoured cars came tearing down the road and stopped outside the house. Out stepped a sergeant in familiar battle dress and beret, he looked around waved to us and opening the rear of the scout car and pulled out an empty water container and then walked towards the house. I opened the door before he knocked in my excitement asked him how many cars were in his unit, 'just us four mate' then he realising I had spoken in English and asked who I was.

I told him and he called back to an officer in one of the cars 'there's a bloody RAF bloke in this house'

Meanwhile it didn't take long for the local people to realise they were almost free of German occupation at last and I have never seen such excitement. They poured out of the houses and gathered around the army Scout cars and orange bunting and flags appeared from bedroom windows. The British soldiers had no alternative but to stop for a quick brew of tea and biscuits with the newly liberated people of Deurne. I was given 100 cigarettes and a mug of real tea with sugar while some of the locals exchanged eggs and milk for tins of army Bully beef.

The unit was an advanced patrol of The Inns of Court Regiment, commonly known as Monty's Greyhounds.

Suddenly the air was shattered by the piercing scream of a shell and earth blew up in field across the road. In a few seconds the scout cars vanished back up the road and we dashed back to the house and went down into the cellar.

The Germans continued to shell the village until about mid-day and then German troops and tanks came down the road. I cannot remember much about the shelling because we settled ourselves in the cellar on some straw and I fell asleep.

It was about 2 o'clock when I woke, German units continued to pour down the road all the afternoon. An hour later another noise started to rend the air and my Dutch friends told me this came from a German Morter battery situated a short distance away at the cross roads.

Just before 4 o'clock three RAF Typhoons flew over and fired their rockets at the Morter position and the village fell silent once again.

The German troops seemed to disappear and we celebrated with a meal of cheese, biscuits, tomatoes and apples washed down with more of that awful coffee. I shared out the carton of cigarettes and finally we all closed our eyes and went to sleep

At first light British troops appeared with tanks and scout cars and the infantry started to dig fox holes and set up machine gun posts, this time the Allies had come to stay.

The news that an RAF sergeant was living in the village must have been passed on, for at about 10am two MPs arrived and said they had orders to take me to their headquarters for interrogation.

I hardly had time to thank my Dutch friends for all their help but I did manage to get Jo's name it was Browers and I gave him my home address, he made one request which I couldn't refuse after all he had done for me, he wanted me to return the Dutch Identification card as a memento.

My journey back was irritating, I was in civilian clothes unshaven, treated as a suspect by the Army, I was interrogated at the Army Headquarters by a Major, 'what was my rank, name and number, what aircraft was I flying? Over and over . There were forms to fill in and then a Colonel arrived and it all started again. I suggest it would be best to take me to the nearest RAF unit and let them establish my identity. I refused to hand over the rest of my escape money, saying I had signed for that at my Base, and it would be returned there. Seeing I was going to be awkward, they put me in a jeep with two MPs and drove to RAF Tactical Air Command Headquarters at Hellmond.

'Name, rank, number' here it all began again, what Squadron, who was my pilot, what was our target, number of aircraft, how had I obtained civilian clothes?

At last I was taken to an office where two officers were present, one was my Skipper S/L Hugh Horsley all dressed up in uniform as if he was going on parade. The other officer turned to him and said 'Do you know this man Squadron Leader?'

My Skipper turned and looked me full in the face and said 'Never seen him before in my life'

The other officer asked in surprise 'Are you sure he says he's your Rear Gunner'

'Well I don't recognise him because I have never seen his face before, he always sits with his back to me in the aircraft'

We all had a good laugh and they congratulated me on my escape. A month later we were back on operations with No 61 Squadron at RAF Skellingthorpe.

On the 1st February 1945 a Lancaster flown by S/L Hugh Horsley crashed on take-off at RAF Skellingthorpe. Sgt Reg Hoskisson was the only survivor.

CHAPTER 15

EVADER

P/O Charles A.Cawthorne DFM

After diving head first through the escape hatch in the bomb aimer's compartment of our Lancaster QR-K, I have no recollection whatsoever of pulling the rip cord but do recall hanging on the end of my parachute and yelling frantically the name of our bomb aimer Johnny Wheeler and expecting him to be only a few hundred yards away.

On reflection, I think my calling was not only in fright but in the realisation that I was alone and in a desperate situation. Somehow while exiting from the plane I had received quite a crack on my skull but under the circumstance this gave me no immediate concern. I recall the absolute quiet except the rushing of air through the parachute shrouds and looking down I thought the ground was coming up fast so I prepared to land. The expected impact didn't come and when I opened my eyes I found that I was falling through swirling cloud. Once through the cloud it really became pitch black and I had no idea of my height above the ground or in fact what country I was about to land in.

Suddenly without warning I hit the ground with a terrific thump and lay there somewhat dazed for a few seconds. I soon recovered from the initial shock and after taking stock of the situation ascertained that while there were no bones broken I did have severe pain in my left leg when I tried to walk. My parachute had snagged on a barbed wire fence so I tried to haul it off but unfortunately it kept billowing up in the wind. After the third attempt to release it I heard dogs barking close by and immediately thought German soldiers would appear any minute. So I abandoned the task of trying to hide my chute and ran wildly across fields in sheer panic as I tried to get as much distance between myself and possible pursuers. While moving blindly along the edge of a field I tripped over some low barbed wire fencing and fell into the ditch and in my state of shock became terrified when some cattle I had disturbed started to stampede across the field. I staggered on and an hour later, utterly exhausted and panic stricken I found a secluded ditch covered in bracken where I decided to rest. Then to my utter amazement I found a rolled up parachute in the ditch so without hesitation, immediately left the area and again travelled over fields to put as much distance between myself and the area where I had landed. Eventually I found a small wood where I hid and gained some rest. There I took stock of my situation and to my horror realised I had lost the package containing local maps and money out of my escape kit.

Throughout the next day I stayed concealed and waited until late evening before venturing out. About half a mile away on the other side of the wood I saw some farm outbuildings. After a cautious approach I found the barn was full of hay and as I had not slept for 48 hours decided to try and get some rest.

The following morning I was in better spirits and decided the best course of action was to try and look like a local farm worker. From my air force jacket I tore off my badges of rank brevet and medal ribbons and then pulled my white flying jersey over the top. Then I thought the jersey was too conspicuous so I decided to darken it with mud and anything else I could find. I then cut off the tops of my flying boots so they looked like ordinary walking shoes. To complete my disguise I found an old hemp sack in the barn which I slung across my shoulders and outside an old green enamel bucket which had a handle but no bottom. This I decided to carry and try to pass myself off as a foreign peasant worker if confronted by the Germans.

At this stage I had no idea where I was so after leaving the barn I headed west keeping close to hedgerows or cautiously walking down narrow country lanes. As night approached I hid in a wood of fir trees and by this time was desperately in need of water. The problem was that I had no container in which to use my purification tablets with the water I found in the ditches. By morning I was becoming very dehydrated and decided it was imperative, whatever the risks, to find water quickly. After moving down the muddy cart track that ran alongside a wood I saw a small cottage with smoke coming from the chimney. After keeping it under observation for a while I saw an elderly lady dressed in a long skirt with a shawl over her shoulders. She came out of the cottage to collect some fire wood from a pile stacked close by the door and then went back inside. In desperation, I picked up a piece of wood to use as an offensive weapon if necessary and approached the door of the cottage. After a brief hesitation I turned the door knob and went inside and saw the old lady sitting in front of the fire. She was alone and I could see that my sudden entrance and unkempt appearance had frightened her. By outlining a parachute with my fingers and then with my forefinger writing RAF, she immediately realised that I was an airman and then became more relaxed and friendly. At this stage of events I didn't even know what nationality she was so I was still very suspicious and on my guard. After indicating that I needed a drink she immediately gave me what I thought was coffee but found that it tasted like turnips and couldn't drink it. She also offered me some very dark bread which tasted like sawdust and some dreadful goat cheese. Although I was most grateful for her generosity I just could not eat anything for want of water. Eventually after further sign language she responded by giving me a drink of cold water from a stoneware jar.

Suddenly without warning a young man of around 16 years of age come into the kitchen and after a hurried conversation with the old lady went into another room. I thought it time to depart but as I made for the door the old lady intervened and pointed to the boy who had just re-entered the room carrying some old clothes. He placed an old cap on my head and helped me on with a short dark coat that covered my bedraggled uniform. I pushed the cap over the back of my head as worn in England but with a severe "Non, Non!" the young man made me put it on the fore part of my head. I must have looked rather ridiculous because the coat was too short to be an overcoat but too long to be a jacket but I did as I was told and we went outside. The young man then took me quite a distance from the cottage and hid me in a small wood that was well away from any roads.

That evening I heard voices and then saw dark figures approaching my hiding place and immediately thought I had been betrayed and the Germans were combing the wood for me. My panic eventually subsided when I saw they were civilians and led by the young man from the cottage. Apparently they were all from a nearby village and I had obviously become the centre of attention. Shortly afterwards they led me down a narrow lane towards a large house with a red panelled front door. After knocking several times, my companions suddenly started talking impatiently amongst themselves and as none of them spoke English I was becoming very unhappy about the situation and in a bit of a quandary about what to do next.

Suddenly the heavy door was opened and we were confronted by a short stout man who spoke in a very aggressive and authoritative way. He issued orders to some of the men who were standing by my side and then proceeded to scrutinise me in a quite unfriendly manner. At the time I thought he was a German official like the Gestapo and wished I had been armed. It later transpired that he was a prominent member of the community and a leader of the local Dutch resistance movement. I was then escorted to another house in the village for a short while before being taken to a Convent where the nuns made me very welcome. After a wash they fed me with fresh eggs, potatoes and black bread. That night I enjoyed the almost forgotten luxury of sleeping in a bed with clean white sheets. Early next morning after thanking the nuns for their kind hospitality we were soon trekking once again across the dykes and flat fields of Holland.

Just before midday my Dutch companions pointed to some army vehicles that were parked under a clump of trees and announced they were British. We waved and shouted to the soldiers as we crossed the field towards them but we didn't receive the kind of welcome that I had expected. One of my companions indicated to the troops that I was British and after bidding me a short farewell soon disappeared in the direction from which we had just come. I gave the NCO in charge of the scouting unit my RAF rank and serial number but was not treated at all well because I was dressed as a civilian and I had no means of identification. When I tried to explain that my aircraft had been shot down and I was an RAF officer they took one look at me and thought it was a huge joke. Evidently the reason for their suspicious attitude was because German troops had, a few days before, infiltrated the British lines dressed as civilians and played havoc with front line communications.

Over the next two days I was passed from one army unit to another, each time I was interrogated but no one seemed to believe my story. Finally I was brought in front of the Commanding Officer, and again I got the impression that he did not believe me. So I decided that enough was enough and swore at him like an old soldier for at least two minutes using every abuse I could muster. When I had finally exhausted my four letter word vocabulary, he said, "Blimey if you can swear like that you must be British". At last I was given a good square meal and later, cigarettes and a bar of chocolate.

The following morning the CO of the army unit gave me the option of staying locally with a Dutch family until that sector of Holland had been liberated or travel with them. It was only then that I fully realised that it was the Dutch who had befriended me and risked so much to ensure my safety. Later I learned our aircraft QR-K had crashed near the village of Deurne in the south east of Holland. As I could not understand the local language I elected to stay with the army unit. I found out later that this same unit, the Inns of Court Reconnaissance Corps, had helped our rear gunner Reg Hoskisson back to the British lines. I travelled in a small armoured car where the driver sat amidships of the vehicle enabling him to drive fast in both forward and reverse directions. It wasn't long before I understood why this facility was necessary.

Later that day we entered a small village and came across some British troops cooking a meal outside a schoolroom. We had just slowed down when there was a terrific explosion in front of us quickly followed by a series of smaller ones. Before I knew what was happening the driver had slammed the vehicle into reverse and soon distanced us from a very dangerous situation. The small explosions I heard were apparently smoke grenades being fired to hide our vehicle from some German tanks that had fired at us. Shortly afterwards the air was alive with low flying RAF Typhoon fighter bombers which soon dispersed the enemy tanks with rockets. Following this exciting episode I was quickly passed back along the British lines and had the great pleasure of being in Brussels a few days after the city had been liberated. Although I was dressed in a mixture of RAF trousers and an Army battledress top I was treated royally by the celebrating Belgians. Eventually an RAF aircraft flew me back to England and after further interrogation in London I was sent on leave and reunited with my family.

On returning to No.61 Squadron at RAF Skellingthorpe I was told the sad news that two of our crew had perished in the crashed aircraft but the good news was that the skipper S/L Hugh Horsley and rear gunner Reg Hoskisson had also evaded and returned to the

Squadron while Johnny Wheeler and Jack Webber were thought to be prisoners of war.

Shortly afterwards I entered hospital to have my damaged left leg re-set and then came a period of rehabilitation and welcome home leave. As soon as I was fully mobile I journeyed up to Johnny Wheeler's parents home and reassure them that Johnny was a prisoner of war in Germany and with a bit of luck would soon be home.

CHAPTER 16

BEHIND THE WIRE

F/O John P.Wheeler

The night fighter attack on QR-K and the following defensive corkscrew tactic was a terrifying experience and when the skipper finally gave the order "Get Out" I quickly ejected the escape hatch in my bomb aimers compartment. In front of me was a black hole through which the slipstream whistled and an occasional flash of light could be seen far below. Time seemed to stand still as the emergency drill ran quickly through my mind;

1 Don't bale out feet first as the slip stream from the aircraft could force the lower part of your body backwards and you could decapitate yourself as you left.
2 Check that your parachute is securely attached to the harness.
3 Head between legs, kneel at the side of the exit and roll out.
4 If sufficient height left, a quick count to ten and deploy the parachute.

After clearing the aircraft the first sign that I might survive the night's traumatic events was the jerk on the parachute harness that indicated the canopy had deployed and I was floating serenely down to earth. Shortly afterwards I experienced an intense feeling of relief that I had managed to get out of the aircraft alive but at the same time wondered how the rest of the crew had fared. In the distance the sky was lit by searchlights and apart from sporadic flak the only noise I heard on the way down was the drone of Lancaster engines high above as the heavy laden bombers continued their way to the target. One advantage of baling out in the dark is that all your muscles are relaxed as you hit the ground and therefore you minimize the chance of injury to your ankles. I landed quite safely in a field full of cabbages.

The main points of the aircrew Escape and Evasion lecture

continued to run through my mind. We were told *"Once on the ground get rid of any evidence as to your whereabouts"*. I quickly rolled up my parachute and harness and looked for somewhere to hide them. Close by I discovered a small pond so without further delay I hid the gear amongst the reeds and then weighted it all down under the water with large stones. I then moved away from my landing area as quickly as I could and hid behind a boundary wall and took stock of my situation.

Fortunately I had managed to get down without losing my flying boots. This was a bonus because I was wearing the older type of suede boot with a zip fastener which were notorious for coming adrift under such circumstances. In order to help me formulate a plan of escape I took out the escape kit from my pocket. Amongst the things in front of me were :-

Small silk maps of the area we were flying over.
Currency - Dutch Guilders, German Marks, French and
Belgian Francs.
Concentrated chocolate bars and Horlicks tablets.
Water purifying tablets.

Also one of my battledress buttons could be converted into a magnetic compass. The top portion of the button unscrewed and when turned over became free moving on its base. In order to evade enemy forces we were advised to walk by night and sleep by day.

As we were flying over Holland when we abandoned the aircraft I decided to try to join up with some of our Airborne forces still fighting in the Arnhem/Nijmegen region. I did not know that the decision to withdraw the Allied troops from Oosterbeek and Nijmegen sector had already been taken and the area was full of German troops.

Capture

I remembered we were flying over the city of Eindhoven when our aircraft was attacked by the night fighter so I estimated my present position to be about 20 miles south of Nijmegen. Feeling confident I set off north and hoped to get my bearings from the next village I came across. Unfortunately it was not to be because as I made my way down a narrow country road I was suddenly accosted by a German soldier who was on guard duty outside a small village. Although I did try to make a break for it without too many histrionics, I was surrounded by German soldiers within a few minutes.

After being searched and relieved of a packet of cigarettes by the guards, I was taken to a forward command post where I was interviewed by a young German officer. He asked me if I had anything to say to which I pointed out that my cigarettes had been removed.

The guard who had them was still with me and he received quite a rollicking from his superior and the cigarettes were returned to me. Thank goodness I had been taken by front-line troops. My school language lessons were becoming very useful enabling me to reply to all questions in German with my name, rank and service number. I also quoted the Geneva Convention of 1926 as to what I was allowed to say as a Prisoner of War.

After a short while I was taken under escort to German Headquarters in a large staff car. When we arrived, the place seemed to be in complete chaos and I began to think and hope that it wouldn't be too long before the Allied troops over-ran this sector. Unfortunately it was not to be and after further questions I was bundled into another staff car which took me at great speed from Arnhem to a civilian jail in Nijemgen. Artillery and small arms fire could still be heard in the vicinity of the Nijmegen Bridge and again my hopes were that I would soon be released by Allied forces. The Dutch prison officers were very kind and there was a great feeling of optimism among them and the local Dutch population. Regrettably it was premature. Two days later I was taken from the jail under armed escort for the journey to the German Luftwaffe interrogation centre at Oberursel near Frankfurt-am-Maine. We joined a column of captured airborne forces from the Arnhem area. Amongst the British and American paratroopers and glider pilots were a few more RAF types and we were all herded into the infamous enclosed rail wagons. Lt.Col McCardie of the South Staffordshire Regiment was the senior British officer present, and we helped him look after the walking wounded until they could be sent to a German hospital. Most of this group had survived ten days of intense fighting around Oosterbeek and I had the utmost admiration for their courage, tenacity and humour.

Upon arrival at the Oberursel interrogation centre we were each allocated a sweat box. Originally designed for solitary confinement, the sweatbox was a small cell the temperature of which was controlled from outside and used to soften up prisoners prior to interrogation. There were however so many prisoners from Arnhem that these solitary cells were holding up to eight PoWs at a time.

The usual methods of interrogation were applied, but fortunately we had been fore-warned of these German methods by our Squadron Intelligence Officer and were prepared. I think the German authorities were embarrassed by the number of prisoners at the centre and after seven days we were on the way to our permanent Kriegsgefangenlager (Prisoner of War Camp).

The following rail journey showed us just how much the Allied bombing campaign had affected the transport system throughout Germany. On our way north we passed through Rheydt/Munchen Gladback, a large rail communications centre which we had bombed a week before and there were still only a couple of lines intact taking any form of traffic.

Later the same day we were attacked by American fighter aircraft. The train suddenly stopped with a jerk and all the German guards jumped off the train and disappeared into the ditches that ran along side the track. Fortunately the strafing attack was not too accurate as we were left locked inside the cattle trucks.

Prisoners arriving at Stalag Luft 1, September 1944

The camp was located near the town of Barth on the Baltic coast some thirty miles west of Stettin. From the camp we could see the test firing of V2 rockets from the area of Peenemünde. It was a typical PoW camp with its posten boxes, barbed and electrical wire, guards, dogs, machine gun posts, and huts raised above the ground so that tunnels could be located more easily. The guard dogs, let loose in the compounds at night were often lured under the huts where they were dosed with a sprinkling of pepper in order to control their ability to pick up scents. Tunnels in the camp went up to 52 with no success. Over the last tunnel attempted in the camp a notice was erected by the German Kommandant with the following words:

R. I. P.
Roses are Red, Violets are blue
This goddam tunnel makes fifty-two

Routine for the day started with the emptying of the barrack blocks by the guards followed by the Appel (roll call). This was in the form of an outdoor parade inside the compound. Depending on how we felt, this could take up to two hours since there were many ways of putting doubt into the mind of the Oberfeldwebel (Regimental Sergeant Major) who was responsible for giving the number of prisoners present to the officer in charge of the parade.

Food Rations

Subject to availability, breakfast consisted of one or two slices of German ersatz black bread. This was a strange concoction. When mixed with water on the fire stove in the room it would cement bricks together!! Lunch and dinner was usually a helping of very watery soup supplied by the Germans from their cook-house, with one slice of bread. Sometimes sauerkraut, turnips and other vegetables were supplied by the Germans but these became very scarce towards the end. Apart from the soup collected from the German kitchen, all our cooking had to be done by ourselves on a coal fired field stove within the room.

If Red Cross parcels were available they supplemented the diet. The contents of a typical British Red Cross Parcel was as follows

1 tin of Nestle's condensed milk
1 packet of prunes or apricots
½ lb of margarine
1 tin of bacon, salmon or pilchards
4 oz of cocoa (Terry's or Rowntree's)
12 oz tin of corned beef or Gallantine
1 cake of soap
4 oz slab of chocolate
1 slab of Tate and Lyle sugar
1 tin of cheese, ½ lb of biscuits
1 lb tin of jam
Creamed rice or fruit pudding
2 oz of tea
1 tin of curried beef
50 cigarettes or 2 oz Tobacco
1 tin of Tate & Lyle syrup

These Red Cross parcels were excellent, but I cannot remember at any stage anyone receiving one parcel per person per week. It was always a shared ration and we received no parcels for three months in the Autumn/Winter of 1944 and none for the last two months of the war.

Morale

Life inside a Prisoner of War camp presents an ideal situation in which to study factors affecting morale. Factors such as the weather, quality and quantity of food, lack of home news and a continuous diet of censored news influenced our day to day outlook on life. However, by using various clandestine methods we did manage to receive the BBC news reports at least once a day. So by comparing the BBC broadcast with the German news service it was possible to keep track of the Allied armies progress during the last six months of the war.

Letters from home

Mail from home became almost non-existent. From my arrival in the camp, in late September 1944, I received no mail until two letters on 25th December and three more in February 1945, one letter in March and one in April. A letter posted in Dover on 28th December 1944 had a stamp on it saying "This letter formed part of undelivered mail which fell into the hands of the Allied Forces in Germany. It is undeliverable as addressed and is therefore returned to you". This was returned to its sender at the end of hostilities in Europe.

Home mail was naturally a great boost to morale, except in some cases where Dear John letters were received. Some letters were humorous and others very sad. A few excerpts are given below:

- If you need any money let me know - to Lieutenant H.B. - from his mother
- I have been living with an army private since you were shot down, but please do not stop my allowance as he does not make as much money as you - to an RAF Sgt from his wife.
- I knew I should have kept you here and joined the Air Corps myself. Even when you were a kid I knew you would end up in prison - to Lieutenant D.M. from his father.
- When and if you return I'd like a divorce. I am living with a cadet and wish to marry him. He's wonderful and I know you'll like him - to Lieutenant V.R. from his wife.
- Do you get to town often where you are? - to Lieutenant M.L. from his wife.

Goon Baiting

The German camp guards were kept busy all day with roll calls and searches for possible escape activity. To the prisoners these unfortunate guards were known as Goons (two pounds of shit in a one pound bag) and were baited constantly by the prisoners from the time they opened up the barrack blocks in the morning until the night shift left. They were also taunted with threats of being posted to the Russian front.

One particularly successful time wasting raid was carried out by the prisoners on the German Administrative Block situated in the Vorlager. Many documents were stolen and destroyed. This resulted in our being locked outside our huts for about eight hours whilst the Goons carried out a massive search. Nothing was ever found.

Occasionally the Germans complained to the British and American senior officers about the use of the word Goon by the prisoners. The following notice was displayed in the camp during July 1944.

Kriegsgefangenlager No.1. Barth den 2.7.1944

de Luftwaffe. Gruppe II

To Senior American Officer North Compound

Senior American Officer South Compound

Senior British Officer South Compound

Re Use of the word GOON

The use of the word Goon was granted to prisoners of war by the Kommandant under the condition that this word would not have any dubious meaning.

It has, however, been reported to me that prisoners have been using the phrase focking goon up, the meaning of which is beyond any doubt. Consequently, the use of the word Goon or Goon up is prohibited, severest punishment being inflicted in future disobedience against this order.

Shroder leiter gcz

V Gruppen. Major

Fuel became very scarce during the winter months. Our bed bunks consisted of straw mattresses on top of wooden slats. These slats of wood provided excellent fuel and by the end of our time in the camp we were sleeping on an average of two slats per bunk.

During a lifetime one meets certain characters who are outstanding, and their qualities remain in your memory. Such a character was Captain the Reverend H A M Mitchell from Dunedin in New Zealand. He was our camp Padre. For a time, before and after Christmas, food was very short and roll calls were eventually taken inside the barrack blocks as many of us were suffering with a degree of malnutrition and quite literally passing out during any form of exertion. It was well known that Capt. The Rev. Mitchell had passed on his very meagre rations to those he thought were in greater need, until one Sunday morning during his sermon he became a victim of these privations and passed out!! The effect of his work, his cheery disposition and simple, very practical faith had a great influence on keeping up the morale of the camp.

At Christmas 1944 he conducted the camp Carol Service. His meticulous organisation down to the printing of the service sheets with the facilities available within the camp had to be experienced to appreciate his untiring energy. The Remembrance Service in November, held on the parade area, was also an example of his indomitable spirit in difficult circumstances. After Christmas 1944, German rations became scarce and Red Cross parcels non-existent and it was not until late March 1945 that there was a slight improvement. The end of the war was now in sight with the Allies as very obvious victors.

Our typical menu for the first four months of 1945 based on German rations, no Red Cross parcels being available, was as follows:

Breakfast	2 slices of toast from German ersatz bread with turnip jam. 1 cup German ersatz coffee
Lunch	1 slice toast with turnip jam 2 slices toast with mashed turnips
Dinner	Stew (?) consisting of German issue soup, potatoes and turnips

Note : by saving bread it was possible to make one cake with no fruit.

Liberation

In April 1945 the Red Army opened up their offensive on Stettin. We became aware of this when the inevitable artillery barrage could be heard.

On 29th April there was a discernible lack of discipline among the German guards. Eleven men were missing from our roll call to which the German Officer-in Charge of the parade just replied the equivalent of "Oh, it doesn't matter a damn". During the morning the Germans carried out the demolition of the apparatus at the flak School that was situated adjacent to the Camp and throughout the day there was a noticeable panic in the Vorlager (German HQ). The goons even gave permission for us to dig slit trenches outside our huts with spades.

There were rumours that the Germans were going to evacuate the camp at any time so we were placed on standby in case we were needed to take over the Posten Boxes from the German sentries.

In the late afternoon an urgent meeting was arranged between the German camp Kommandant Colonel Warnstedt, the senior British officer Group Captain Weir and the senior American officer Colonel Zemke. The Kommandant stated that he had received orders to move the whole camp westward. Colonel Zemke stated that he was not prepared to move at all and asked what the German response would be to such a refusal.

The Kommandant replied that he would not tolerate any bloodshed inside the camp. Furthermore, if we did not intend to move, he and his men would evacuate themselves and leave us in sole possession of the camp.

At approximately 01.30 hours on the 30th April, Major Steinhauer informed Group Captain Weir and Colonel Zemke that the Germans had evacuated the camp, leaving it in their charge. A few hours later the rest of camp woke up to find that the German guards had all discreetly disappeared and they were no longer under armed guard and comparatively free. As soon as it was light a scouting party consisting of Major Braithwaite and Sgt Korson set out to try and make contact with the advancing Russians. This they did and at 22.25 hours Lt Alec Nick Karmyzoff and his driver arrived in a lorry at the main gate.

After a back slapping welcome by Commanding Officers Weir and

Zemke they went into the Kommandant's office and consumed a number of throat burning Schnapps in toasts of "Friendship between the Allies" and the total "Destruction of Nazi Germany".

The Russians arrived in full force on 2nd May and then quickly set about making the area secure and assessing the needs of the prisoners inside the camp. Adjacent to our camp was a Luftwaffe airfield and within its perimeter they found a fenced off accommodation block that housed several hundred forced labour workers. Four men, one Russian, one Hungarian and two Poles were found to be in a terrible state and immediately taken to our sick quarters for treatment.

With permission from the Russian Commander, Stalag Luft 1 was thrown open and we were able to go outside the camp for the first time since the German guards left. My friend, Jack Louden, and I took the opportunity to stretch our legs and walked over to the far side of the Barth peninsula.

Everywhere we went the Russian soldiers welcomed us with open arms and it was quite a reassuring sight to see the Red Army moving slowly through the town of Barth in an odd assortment of requisitioned vehicles. The joy of our newly obtained freedom was somewhat tainted when we came across five German dead bodies, including a baby in a pram.

The following day we were under full Russian Command and for our own safety martial law was introduced.

On the 4th May the Russian senior officer, Colonel Zchervynick, announced that Berlin was now in the hands of the Russian army and the long awaited link-up with the Western Allies had been achieved. As if in celebration two American Thunderbolts from Colonel Zemke's old 56th Fighter Group flew over in the late afternoon.

The following day the Russian field commander, Marshal Rokatofski, visited the camp and a parade was given in his honour.

The first American front line troops arrived at around 16.00 hours and news quickly spread throughout the American and British compounds that they had brought detailed plans of a fast repatriation programme.

During one of our walks outside the camp we visited the labour camp on the nearby airfield and found an unbelievable state of affairs. The inmates were living in filthy conditions and many of them had been without food and water for the last four days. Hospitalisation for the sick was underway and assessments were being carried out by Russian, British, French and Czech doctors. Lice and skin disease was widespread amongst the inmates and eighty-five of the poor devils were found to be suffering from tuberculosis, malnutrition and dysentery and almost beyond help.

On 6th May the Russians drove pigs and cattle into one of the compounds. Slaughter houses were quickly set up in the wood and fresh meat was assured at the camp for the rest of our stay. Some of the PoWs even supplemented their rations by catching fish in the nearby Baltic inlet. The following day we were told Nazi Germany had surrendered and all hostilities would end at midnight.

To help us celebrate this marvellous news the Russian equivalent of an E N S A show arrived at the camp with three girl entertainers, a military band and Cossack dancers. Later a Russian news film of the Yalta Conference was screened and also a comedy short based on German's offensive in Russia.

While we waited patiently for our turn to be repatriated, a daily news sheet was produced to keep us informed about what was going on.

The same team of would be newspaper reporters set about publishing the one and only issue of a camp newsletter called the BARTH HARD TIMES. It was issued on 5th May 1945 and the headline read;

TENSE MOMENTS WHILE THE ALLIES TAKE CONTROL

by War Correspondent Lowell Bennet

"An air of tension hung over the camp for many days. The presence of the English and American armies on the Elbe and the Russian encirclement of Berlin made everyone feel that the end must be near.

The commencement of a new Russian drive across the lower Oder towards the Baltic ports finally increased the tension to an almost unbearable pitch.

Panic reigned in the Vorlager. No German had any more interest in guarding the prisoners, but only in saving his own life.

Confidential reports were hurriedly burnt and even copies of Hitler's book Mein Kampf went to swell the flames."

BARTH

HARD TIMES

Vol 1 No. 1 LAST 1 SATURDAY MAY 5th 1945 PRICE 1 D- BAR.

Editor: F/L E. R. INKPEN Assoc: 1st Lt N. GIDDINGS Publisher: 1st Lt D. MacDONALD Printing: F/LT J. D. WHITE

RUSSKY COME!

As seen by LOWELL BENNET, I. N. S. War Correspondent.

WHAT D'YE KNOW- JOE!!

RELIEVED!

Colonel Zemke intended to write this appreciation of the relief of Stalag Luft I, but unfortunately necessary duties have made this impossible. He has, in his own words, "taken a powder" to make final arrangements with the relieving Soviet forces.

It is therefore my privilege to introduce this Memorial Edition of the BARTH HARD TIMES.

During the successes, reverses and stagnant periods encountered during this struggle, our newspaper has faithfully recorded the German war communiques and expanded upon them in capable editorials.

With the redemption of a continent, our exile is ended. Our barb-bound community will soon be a memory. So, on behalf of Colonel Hubert Zemke and myself, to all our fellow-kriegies: GOOD LUCK!

G./C. C. T. Weir.

BRAITHWAITE FINDS UNCLE JOE

Contacts Russian Infantryman at Crossroads Five miles South of Stalag One.

Major Braithwaite and Sgt Korson, our Stalag scouts, raced out to a cross-roads 5 miles south of Barth with the order, "find Uncle Joe". This was 8 p. m., May 1.

They searched southward, defying a rumored Russian curfew which was about as brief and emphatic as their own order: "EVERYONE stay put; anyone seen moving will be shot on sight."

Meanwhile, Wing Commander Blackburn's telephone crew were ringing numbers in Stralound, hoping a Russian would answer the phone and we could break the big news of our presence. "Try the mayor," they asked the girl (who was still working Barth's phone exchange). "Not a chance," said she. "Barth's mayor poisoned himself and Stralsund's mayor has sprouted wings."

Scouts Braithwaite and Korson pushed on 3 miles. The scenery: thousands of people everywhere, sitting down, waiting.

LIFE AND DEATH OF A GERMAN TOWN

TENSE MOMENTS WHILE ALLIES TAKE CONTROL

An air of tension hung over the camp for many days. The presence of the English and American armies on the Elbe and the Russian encirclement of Berlin made everyone feel that the end must be near. The commencement of a new Russian drive across the lower Oder toward the Baltic ports finally increased the tension to an almost unbearable pitch. Panic reigned in the Vorlager. No German had any more interest in guarding the prisoners, but only in saving his own life. Confidential reports were hurriedly burnt — and copies of "Mein Kampf" went to swell the flames.

Conference with the Kommandant

Finally, late in the afternoon, the Senior British and American officers were called to a conference with the German camp Kommandant Colonel Warnstedt. They were told that orders had been received to move the whole camp westward. Colonel Zemke stated he was not willing to move at all, and asked in that case what the German attitude would be. The Commandant replied that he would not tolerate bloodshed in the camp; if we did not intend to move, he and his men would evacuate themselves and leave us in sole possession of the camp. When the Germans left it would be up to us to take over the camp peacefully and assume full control.

At approximately 1 A.M. on April 30 Major Steinhauer informed Group Captain Weir and Colonel Zemke that the Germans had evacuated the camp, leaving it in our charge. When the camp woke up in the morning it was to find itself no longer under armed guard and comparatively free.

Where are the Russians?

Our next problem was to establish contact with the Russian forces. It was decided to send out something in the nature of a recco patrol. An American Major, a British Officer speaking German, and an American Officer speaking Russian, set out with the German in the auto which was equipped with an American flag on one fender and a white flag on the other, to investigate the real situation in Barth and then proceed to the main Stralsund—Rostock road, some 15 kilometers south of the camp, to wait there for any signs of Russian spearheads or of the proximity of the front line. The first patrol returned in the early evening. Still no sign or news of the Russian Army, but they were coming!

Russian Contact (con. from Page 1)

Every house draped with red flags (who said the Germans weren't chameleons?). Suddenly, there was Uncle Joe — — or one of his ambassadors: a chunky little Dead End guy who loomed up and flashed a variety of lethal weapons and a cacophony of Slavic language.

"Engliski", shouted the scouts.

"Never mind the words", said Joe's man, "this isn't Dulag" or something like that in Russian. And, without ceremony they went to the nearest Russian officer. It was 1st Lt. Alec Nick Karmyzoff, infantryman from Tula (you oughta see that written in Russian!) He'd fought his way from Stalingrad — three years across Russia, Poland and Germany — to the relief of Stalag Luft I.

Toasts are Drunk.

Karmyzoff came in the main gate. Commanding Officers Zemke and Weir received him. Schnapps seared kriegie throats — glasses smashed Hitler's picture, the barracks jiggled with cheering and back-pounding. Toasts were drunk: " To the destruction of Germany — she will never rise again! And to our solid and enduring friendship." Karmyzoff went to the Russian barracks (our co-kriegies) — told them about himself, their army and the new life that was beginning. Thus the first contact. Karmyzoff bedded down on the floor — "Rather the floor than a German bed," said he. BBC announced Hitler dead; kriegies heard the "Hit Parade" from home; the excitement was exhausting. — But what an experience!

QUAKING BARTH BURGHERS BOW BEFORE REDS

As Russian tanks rumbled Northwards on the cobblestone roads from Stralsund, as Russian cavalry and guerilla troops tore hell bent for the Baltic, as the spluttering German radio flashed a staccato of place names that had gone under in the Red rip tide, Barth became an open city and an open grave. The few Americans who had been in town on camp chores from Stalag I knew that the life of Barth was a living death. We had seen the streets peopled by children and octogenerians, we had noticed that all males were either lame, halt, or blind; we had stared into empty shop windows, and we had seen the soldiers of the master race straggle back from the fronts dazed, whipped, harbingers of the ruin that stalked the streets of German towns. By April 30, this year of grace, the good burghers of Barth turned their faces to the wall and stopped hoping.

LET 'EM EAT CAKE

Life had not been good. In the bakery shop where the camp brot was made hung a sign; cake is not sold to Jews or Poles. It failed to explain that cake was not sold to the supermen either. There was no cake. But there were good things to eat in the larders of Barth, baking powder requisitioned from Holland, Nestles milk commandeered from Denmark, wines looted from the cellars of France, spaghetti and noodles hi—jacked from Italy, Worcestershire sauce which had trickled through mysteriously from England, olive oil drained from Greece, in short, all types of blood from the turnip of Europe. If Mussolini considered the Mediterranean his sea, Hitler considered the world his oyster and was trying to serve it up to the Reich on the half shell.

A House of Cards

As the first explosions from the flak school reverberated under the sullen Baltic sky, the new order toppled on Barth like a house of cards. Red flags and white sheets began to appear in the windows of the ginger bread houses. Flight was futile and the old stood querously on their door steps, wringing gnarled hands and weeping. Pictures of Hitler were torn down and scattered like confetti. Two German children came wailing into the bakery shop. They had heard American airmen ate little boys and mother said the day of reckoning was at hand.

Barth, like the whole of Deutschland-über-alles Germany, was on its knees in terror. But mayhem did not materialize. Wine, not blood, flowed through the streets. We got drunk.

Repatriation

It was a great relief to everyone in the camp that the war was finally over and our Barb-Bound existence in Stalag Luft 1 was about to come to an end. For me and the rest of my long suffering comrades the end of the war meant we had survived and could at last go home to our families.

The end of my eight month incarceration came in the last week of May thanks to the Russian army and the organisers of Operation Exodus. This repatriation operation was quickly initiated at the end of hostilities to fly American, British and Commonwealth prisoners of war back to England. I returned aboard a Flying Fortress of the US 8th Air Force who had joined RAF Bomber Command in flying hundreds of shuttle sorties between the continent and the UK.

All returning prisoners of war were first taken to a holding camp to be medically examined and assessed for further duty. After a thorough examination the doctors diagnosed, not surprisingly, that I was suffering from slight malnutrition and much to my surprise this condition enabled me to qualify for an expectant mother's ration card.

The following few weeks were spent on leave with my family and sometimes I joined the queues of rather rotund ladies collecting extra milk, butter and eggs.

CHAPTER 17

TAIL END CHARLIE

Sgt James W.Boynton

In the spring of 1943 I was a Lancaster rear gunner with No.156 Squadron and flew a Pathfinder tour of ops with F/Lt RE Young and crew from RAF Warboys near Huntingdon. For ten of those operations during the battle of the Ruhr and Hamburg we flew in Lancaster ED860, Squadron code GT-N Nan. In early August the Squadron started to receive aircraft fitted with the new blind bombing equipment H2S and so Nan was transferred to No.61 Squadron after surviving 25 hazardous Pathfinder operations. Little did we know that she was a lucky aircraft and would go on to complete a further 105 ops over the following year as QR-N. At Warboys it was usually about 11 o'clock in the morning that word got around the station that ops were on for the following night. Aircrew looked for their names on the Ops Battle Order that was posted in the Squadron office. Some names appeared on the list despite having been on ops the previous night and not landing back at base until six or seven that morning. These crews had to be awakened by the billet orderlies at mid-day in order for them to prepare for the coming operation.

After a mid-day lunch, our crew would meet in the aircrew locker room, draw our chutes and then board the crew bus which took us out to our aircraft's dispersal. Once the ground crew had completed the aircraft's daily inspections and dealt with any problems reported from the previous operation, we took her up on a night flying test (NFT). This usually lasted about an hour and consisted of each crew member checking over all his operational equipment and making sure everything was working correctly.

The skipper would fly out over the north Norfolk coast to the coastal inlet called the Wash. After checking the area for shipping, we would drop a flame float target into the sea and fire off a few hundred rounds to make sure the eight Browning .303 machine guns were working properly. It also provided good gunnery practice. After returning to base and taxying the aircraft to its dispersal, the petrol bowser would arrive and the ground crew would begin to fill the aircraft's petrol tanks and the armourers set about loading the correct Target Indicators (TIs) and bomb load aboard the aircraft for the coming operation.

If we had had a rough week doing a few ops on the trot, the Medical Officer (MO) would issue us with Wakey, Wakey pills to keep us awake and alert during the long flight. However, we never took them until the very last moment because sometimes the op was scrubbed just before take-off due to dodgy weather en-route, which meant another sleepless night if we had taken a pill too early.

During the early months of 1943, operational briefings were usually held at 16.00 hours. The actual take-off times depended upon the distance to the target, weather and the rise and setting of the moon. After specialist briefings all the aircrews came together in the Squadron briefing room. At the far end of the room a large map of western Europe displayed, with thick red tapes, the route to and from the target.

When everyone was settled, the station commander arrived and various officers gave us the gen on the nights operation. The Flying Control officer gave us times of take-off in aircraft order. Next the Intelligence officer described the route out and home, the time to open the attack with our marker flares and where they were to be placed in the target area. Sometimes we would be briefed to drop markers en-route to keep the main force on the correct path away from heavy flak. Bitter experience had shown that anyone wandering off track 15 or 20 miles would almost certainly become a sitting duck for both fighters and flak. The Squadron Commander then briefed us on where the most flak and fighters were likely to be encountered, lastly the Met man would give us his weather forecast en-route, over the target and for our return in the early hours. Unfortunately he usually got it wrong somewhere along the way, resulting in some of the experienced crews taking the mickey out of him by shouting out "Was your seaweed wet or dry today?" such banter helped to relieved the tension. All the pilots and navigators would set their watches on the time check, the station commander would wish us luck and the briefing was over.

This was followed by a pre-op meal and then we would all try and relax until about an hour and half before take-off when the whole crew would meet up again in the locker room. There we collected all our flying gear including our chutes, Mae West, helmets, flying boots, silk under gloves and gauntlets.

In addition, because of the intense cold experienced in Lancaster rear turrets, gunners were issued with special electrically heated clothing which included an overall, gloves and slippers that fitted inside flying boots. All of which offered some welcome comfort and protection against the extremely low temperatures encountered above 10,000 feet. However, on hot summer nights I never got fully dressed in my flying gear until the aircraft had climbed to a cooler altitude. If I had dressed up in my full flying kit on the ground my perspiration would have frozen on me once airborne. After kitting out we went by crew bus out to the aircraft which was by then bombed up and ready to go.

On take-off there was always a small crowd of officers, WAAFs and airmen to wave us off. While on the take-off run I always turned the rear turret facing the port beam with the turret back doors open just in case of a ground loop crash. In many such accidents the rear gunner often came off the best as the aircraft's main beam area took most of the impact.

At around 6,000 feet I left the turret, got fully dressed and then climbed back in to settle down to concentrate on the task ahead. Later, when I started to feel cold I'd plug my electrically heated suit into the aircraft's power supply.

We had climbed to our operational height of 20,000 feet by the time we reached the coast and, sometimes on a clear starlit night, I would watch the Norfolk shore line rapidly fade into the distance and wonder if we would ever see it again.

Over the North Sea our skipper always flew straight and level until the enemy coast was sighted by the bomb aimer. After that it was weaving all the way to the target. In our opinion to fly straight and level over enemy territory was just plain suicide for a slow heavily laden bomber.

At our first crew meeting the skipper said he believed the only way to survive a tour of forty Pathfinder operations was to have a well disciplined and highly trained crew and a big slice of all the luck going.

After completing a few operations we realised that we would

encounter more heavy flak areas the deeper we penetrated German air space. So the procedure we adopted to counter the German predicted flak batteries, was to fly in an irregular pattern by descending 500-600 feet and then climbing slowly back and also weaving from left to right of the set course. The whole crew, apart from the navigator, were on fighter and friendly aircraft collision watch. The gun turrets on our aircraft never stopped moving from side to side for the duration of the operation. This constant movement and scanning the sky made our aircraft a hard target for both German night fighters and ground defences.

Once over enemy territory many aircraft would be seen going down in flames on the way to the target. Those I actually saw crash on the ground I reported to the navigator giving him their approximate position, he then plotted them on his chart. On some deep penetration operations over Germany, I saw a dozen or more aircraft go down behind us and many more burning on the ground.

One of the most hated anti-bomber defences employed by the Germans was parachute flares dropped by high flying Ju 88 night fighters. These flares would burst just below the bomber stream and illuminate the whole area thus presenting many bombers as silhouetted targets for the night fighters waiting above.

These flares burned so brightly that it was like driving down a well lit road at night and temporarily blinded anyone who was close by. In such circumstances there was nothing the skipper could do apart from weave more violently than usual and try to fly out of range.

The same applied when we got ourselves coned in searchlights. Most large city targets, such as Berlin, had a radar controlled master beam which was blue in colour. If it locked onto an aircraft, another ten to fifteen searchlight beams quickly latched onto the victim who became a sitting duck for the heavy flak batteries. Experienced bomber crews found the only way to escape the master beam was to dive away from the expected flak barrage coming up from below. The last 20 miles to the target had to be flown straight and level in order to make sure target indicators and bombs were placed accurately on the target aiming point. This was a really dodgy period and we were lucky if we were not hit by something or other. Many aircraft were lost at this point, some in collisions and others hit by bombs from above. Sterling and Halifax bombers could only reach about 17,000 feet so they got the lot, the small flak as well as the heavy, plus more attention from the night fighters.

Whilst over the target area, I would often see the fighters attacking bombers silhouetted against the fires on the ground. However, once away from the brightly lit area identifying a fighter was not easy against a black sky. The German night fighter always had the advantage over the bombers and very few were shot down by bomber crews.

It was always a great relief when the bomb aimer said "Bombs gone". The aircraft would rear up and wobble as the weight of the bombs left the aircraft, then we knew all we had to do was go home but that could be nearly as bad as getting there. The route home would be more or less straight apart from trying to avoid any known well defended areas. On some nights if conditions were right the skipper would climb to 27,000 feet then put the nose down and really belt for home. The only snag being that by flying so high the temperature outside was sometimes as low as 60 below freezing. This froze the anti-freeze in the pipes that fired the guns in the rear turret making them useless until they thawed out at a lower altitude. However, the mid-upper guns were electrically fired so were not affected.

Once we had crossed the enemy coast and were well out over the North Sea the skipper would bring us down to 10,000 feet, below oxygen-using height. Everything would then start to warm up and we could relax a little more.

Tommy Evans the bomb aimer would come to the rear turret and bring me a flask of coffee and although smoking was banned while flying, many of us broke that rule. After all the operational stress we had suffered over the past few hours, that mug of coffee and a Woodbine went down really well. I personally always carried a good supply of baccy and a well-filled petrol lighter, just in case we were shot down and managed to get on the run for a while.

On odd occasions a message would come from base that Bandits (enemy fighters) were suspected of being in the area. That meant no relaxation until we were actually back over base. We would then be given a height at which to circle the airfield and a landing number. When our turn came Air Traffic Control radioed permission to land and once down the skipper taxied the aircraft around the perimeter track to our dispersal and we were welcomed back by our ground crew before being picked up by the crew bus and taken to the locker room.

After handing in our flying gear we then went along to the debriefing room were a WAAF officer served us with a mug of coffee well laced with rum and the Padre would hand sandwiches around.

Then we would sit around a table with an intelligence officer and debriefing would begin. "Did you have any difficulty finding the target? At what time were the TIs placed on the aiming point? How heavy was the flak? Did you encounter any fighters? Did you see any aircraft shot down? How far from the target could the fires be seen?" and many other such questions until he had all the information we could give.

Next we collected our personal belongings, including a brown envelope containing our wills and last letters home. These had been deposited and locked away in the Squadron office, for safe keeping before take-off. After that we went to the Mess for an aircrew breakfast before seeking out our billet in a state of utter exhaustion. Hopefully we could get a good mornings sleep before being called once again to go to war.

CHAPTER 18

TALES FROM THE SQUADRON

Duty Calls

At RAF Coningsby in the spring of 1944, the regular skipper of Lancaster ED860 QR-N Nan, P/O EA Stone was about to go on leave to his home in Bridgewater Somerset.

Just before he and his crew left camp Ted Stone was called into the C/O's office and asked to delay their leave for 24 hours and fly the forthcoming Maximum Effort operation.

In return, the C/O promised to arrange for a sprog crew to fly Ted to the nearest airfield to his home, upon his return to Coningsby the following morning.

After what turned out to be a pretty uneventful operation for the crew, QR-N touched down safely at 06.27 hours and by mid-morning Ted Stone was home.

This maximum effort operation for which the Stone crew delayed their leave was the notorious Nuremberg raid that took place on 30th-31st March 1944. On this night Bomber Command lost their highest number of aircraft during a single operation when ninety-five aircraft failed to return and another fifteen crashed while attempting to land at their bases in England.

Courage

At about 18.30 hours one winter evening in early 1944 ops were on at RAF Coningsby. Three Lancasters had already taken off with a fourth gathering speed half way down the runway when its undercarriage collapsed and as it slewed to a halt on the grass at the side of the runway it burst into flames. Immediately a Red Very went up from the air traffic caravan and all the remaining aircraft stopped on the perimeter track.

The aircrew in the long line of waiting aircraft looked out towards the burning Lancaster and hoped the crew had managed to escape uninjured from the horrendous crash. Their second concern was for their own safety. Would the notoriously unstable 4000 lb Cookie explode and set off the rest of the bomb load thus causing widespread damage. To the waiting crews the delay seemed to last for ages.

In fact only five minutes had passed before a green Very light went up from the control tower and the line of Lancs started moving forward again, much to the relief of all the flight engineers who were becoming concerned about their aircraft engines overheating.

It was impossible for the pilots, bomb aimers and flight engineers in the aircraft to turn their eyes away from the distant inferno. As each aircraft turned onto the runway the scene ahead made the crews very anxious and everyone prayed that the burning Lancaster's bomb load would not blow up as they passed during their take-off run. It took great courage and determination for the remaining Lancaster crews to commit themselves to take-off in such a dangerous situation and then face the Berlin flak and night fighters in the skies over Germany.

Airmanship

An accident recalled by many ex-squadron personnel concerned the demise of Squadron Leader Hugh W.Horsley AFC. This accident was reported in the Lancaster log as:

No.61 Squadron Lancaster NF912 crashed on take-off from RAF Skellingthorpe for Siegen 1st February 1945.

This short entry detracts from a fine piece of airmanship displayed by S/L Horsley in trying to save the lives of his crew. W/O Henry Pyke (E), F/S S Fleet (N), F/S Victor Merrow (BA), F/S Leslie Chapman CGM (W/op), F/S Arthur Sherriff DFM (MUG) and Sgt Reg Hoskisson (RG).

No.50 and No.61 Squadron aircraft started to take-off for Siegen at around 15.15 hours. As usual a large number of Squadron personnel were standing by the flying control caravan, at the end of the runway, to cheer the kites off.

At 15.42 hours Hugh Horsley taxied Lancaster NF912 onto the runway, received a green light from the flying control caravan and after he opened up the four engines the aircraft soon gathered speed and lifted off in a steady climb. The aircraft climbed to about 500 feet when some of the onlookers noticed the propeller on the port outer engine had been feathered. This was quickly followed by the feathering of props on the remaining three engines.

The powerless aircraft was now in a slow diving turn heading back over the airfield. As it rapidly lost height it just managed to skim over QR-P Peter which was still in its dispersal, before making what seemed like a perfect wheels up landing in the overshoot area at the end of the main runway.

Shortly afterwards tragedy struck when the underside of S/L Horsley's aircraft collapsed under the weight of fuel and bombs as it skidded along the runway. Within seconds the friction detonated the unstable thin skinned 4000 lb Cookie and this in turn detonated the remainder of the bomb load. This resulted in a blinding flash followed by a loud explosion which resonated around the airfield. Some of the watching ground staff started to run towards the crash site to see if they could help the crew. When they got there they found a huge crater. The aircraft had broken up into small pieces of distorted metal scattered over a large area, except for the engines and the rear turret which was laying on its side a short distance away from the crater. By this time the station emergency services had arrived on the scene and found to their amazement the rear gunner, Sgt Reg Hoskisson was still alive sitting in his turret. As the fireman carefully extracted him from the wreckage, his first concern was for the rest of his crew. He was then taken to hospital suffering from severe shock and a piece of shrapnel embedded in his back. S/L Horsley and Sgt.Hoskisson had flown together many times. Both had recently returned to the Squadron to continue their tour of operations after being shot down in Lancaster LM718 QR-K on the night of 23rd-24th September 1944 and both had managed to evade capture in Holland until the area was liberated by the advancing Allied army.

Sgt Reg Hoskisson was the only survivor of the crash. Mid-upper gunner F/S Arthur Sherriff DFM was a second tour man and died while acting as a replacement for a sick member of the Horsley crew.

Dishonour and Deterrent

At RAF Syerston one day in October 1943 personnel of No.61 and No.106 Squadron's learned the meaning of the serious charge LMF (Lack of Moral Fibre). Everyone was told to report to the station parade ground at 11.00 hours. They didn't know what was happening as they were formed up into a very ragged three sides of a hollow square in front of the RAF Standard. Suddenly a drum started to beat and a bare headed sergeant with a Military Police escort was marched to the middle of the fourth side of the assembly.

A senior officer moved forward in front of the prisoner and read out a charge of Desertion. Without another word the officer took two steps forward and stopped in front of the poor wretch and then proceeded to pull off his flight engineers brevet, his sergeant stripes and finally the brass buttons on his jacket. Throughout this display of cruel humiliation the drum kept beating, then the prisoner was marched quickly off the parade ground under escort to start his punishment.

Many of the young aircrew who witnessed this ritual of being Drummed Out of the Squadron found the spectacle a very heart-rending experience.

The parade was dismissed and many walked away in silence to reflect on what they had just seen and wonder why they had volunteered for aircrew duties.

Bravery

On the night of 24th February 1945 No.61 Squadron Lancasters took off as part of a 5 Group main force to breach the Dortmund-Ems canal near Ladbergen in northern Germany. However, due to 10/10ths cloud over the target, the Master Bomber decided to abort the operation and the crews were instructed to return to base with some of the bombs. These were mainly 1000 lb HEs fitted with delay fuses and it had always been considered too dangerous to bring this type of bomb back. After jettisoning some of their bomb load in the North Sea to relieve the weight on the aircraft when landing, the Lancasters headed back to their Lincolnshire bases.

An hour later the aircraft of No.61 Squadron joined the Skellingthorpe circuit waiting to be called in to land by Flying Control. Suddenly many of the aircrew in the circling Lancasters saw a large flash on the ground indicating an explosion had taken place on the airfield. Within a few minutes Skellingthorpe was closed down to air traffic and the waiting Lancasters were diverted to land at nearby RAF Waddington. After landing at Waddington all the Squadron aircraft were shepherded to the farthest corner of the airfield and widely dispersed away from all buildings and other aircraft. The aircrews were then ordered to leave their aircraft as fast as possible and were taken away to a debriefing hut to await further instructions. The emergency diversion from Skellingthorpe was the result of Lancaster QR-E Easy landing heavily which activated the short delay fuse in one of the bombs on board. After returning from the abortive operation, QR-E Easy had been parked with other aircraft in line around the perimeter track. The aircrews were quickly taken away for debriefing leaving ground crews working inside and around the aircraft.

Suddenly there was a massive explosion as the whole of E Easy's bomb load went up and completely destroyed the aircraft and damaged several others close by. The initial fear was that the bombs inside the damaged aircraft would also be activated causing a chain reaction. The Squadron armament officer F/Lt Stewart was quickly driven out to take charge of the situation by the B Flight Commander S/L Ian Fadden. They found a large area of devastation all lit up by burning fuel. The station's emergency services were quickly on the scene and dealing with numerous fires and taking the injured to the station sick quarters. The initial casualty report was three dead and many more injured.

After taking stock of the overall situation and talking to the armourers, F/Lt Stewart went along to each aircraft forcing open the bomb doors and defusing all the suspect bombs. For this act of extreme bravery F/Lt Stewart was not even mentioned in dispatches. As one of the Squadron erks said later "There aint no bloody justice".

The three airmen who died in QR-E were LAC B.Burnell, LAC C.H.Higgins and LAC H.G.Wilson.

Discipline and Humour

Two air gunners were on a charge and up before RAF Coningsby's Station Commander. He asked the first sergeant "what did you do in civvy street?". He replied "I was a messenger boy, sir". The second sergeant was then asked the same question "I was a butcher's boy sir". The Group Captain looked down his nose at them and said "What is happening to the Royal Air Force, taking on such uneducated men to fly?".

Needless to say such snobbish comments were not appreciated by the three flight sergeant escorts who rushed back to the sergeants' mess and repeated the CO's comments. The Squadron did not fly any ops for the next two days so it allowed the aircrews time to catch up on some odd jobs and also repaint some of the pictures displayed on many of the aircraft noses.

The following day, as was the practice during operational take-offs, the Station Commander stood at the side of the runway along with many WAAFs and ground staff to wave the aircraft off. The C/O would salute each aircraft as the Aldis lamp flashed on the nose to show its Squadron code letter. This time the lamp showed one aircraft after another with newly painted pictures of Messenger Boys on bicycles with front carriers. Some had newspapers spilling out of their carriers while others showed strings of sausages. Below each piece of nose art was written The Messenger Boys Revenge. The C/O didn't appreciate the joke and as each aircraft took off his face got redder and redder before he finally stalked off in a temper. The next day no operation was laid on, but the call went out for all aircrews to report to their flight hut in full flying kit where they were told that the Station Commander considered them flabby and they were ordered to march around the perimeter track three times and in future physical training would be laid on each day.

The next morning over two thirds of the Squadron joined the sick parade complaining of blisters on their feet. Fortunately for the Station Commander there was an operational stand down for two days or he would have had three quarters of his crews unfit for duty. Needless to say no more was heard about PT.

While Coningsby's Station Commander displayed pre-war attitudes regarding aircrew status, he was a good officer who led from the front and insisted flying on many deep penetration operations over Germany. He failed to return from one of these a few months later.

Inexperienced

The wireless operator of a sprog crew recalls the start of his crew's second operation.

"Our young Aussie pilot was rather inexperienced and this was his first night take-off in a Lanc with a full load on board. We had just reached about 65 mph on our take-off run when the plane started to swing to port, apparently this was a common fault with Lancs. The skipper attempted to correct this with the engines, but was too late.

As we went over the flare path a tyre punctured and the undercarriage collapsed. After that there was nothing anyone could do except pray like mad and hope the detonators in the bombs were robust enough to stand rough treatment and the petrol from the ruptured fuel tanks didn't catch fire. By a miracle we survived. To be fair to the skipper he did remain calm and asked me to fire a Red Very cartridge to warn following planes and then quickly countermanded this order because of the fire risk". "You learn by your mistakes, if you get away with it the first time".

Near Miss Over Lille

On the 10th May 1944, the crew of Lancaster ND898 QR-Q were part of a No.5 Group force attacking the marshalling yards at Lille in France. After releasing their bombs skipper, Reg Dear, held Queenie straight and level for the aiming point photograph. Suddenly while rotating his rear turret Jim Johnson saw the black shape of another Lancaster loom out of the darkness on a collision course. Jim froze in horror expecting the worst as the whirling props of the other aircraft came nearer but at the very last moment the other pilot took avoiding action by lifting his port wing and moving across to starboard. Unfortunately his efforts were too late to prevent his aircraft's port outer propeller slicing two feet off Queenie's port tail fin and rudder. The rear turret gun barrels were also damaged. The impact made Reg Dear's rudder pedals oscillate wildly and this was shortly followed by a phlegmatic report over the aircraft's intercom from his shocked rear gunner "I think we have been hit by another Lanc skipper". Flight engineer, Fred Charlton, was then sent to the rear of the aircraft to make sure the rear gunner was unhurt and investigate the full extent of the damage to the tail fins. Meanwhile Reg cautiously made a gentle turn away from the crowded target area and flew the less responsive Queenie back to Skellingthorpe.

Ground Crew

One of No.61 Squadron B flight NCO's during 1943-45 was Yorkshireman Corporal Ellis Ainley. He was responsible for the serviceability of the engines on Lancasters QR-N Nan QR-Q Queenie, QR-W Willy and QR-X X-Ray.

While at RAF Skellingthorpe these four aircraft had been allocated dispersals on the southern boundary of the airfield near the Squadron hangar and isolated from other dispersals by the main runway.

QR-N Nan by the summer of 1944 was the pride of the Squadron with over 100 ops to her name and engine fitters Sadler and Atkinson resented anyone else looking after her engines. In fact all the Squadron erks took great pride in their work and regarded the aircraft they were assigned to as theirs while it was on the ground and would not let anyone else have a hand in preparing it for operations. The message 'ops on' usually came to the flight dispersals around noon. By which time daily inspections had been done on all the aircraft and any faults found and reported by the aircrew had been dealt with. After satisfying themselves that all the tasks had been completed the various trade NCOs signed the servicing Form 700 signifying the aircraft was fully serviceable and ready to go to war. While all this activity was going on the aircrews would come down to the dispersal to have a look around the aircraft and chat with the ground crew to make sure everything was in working order and, if necessary, take the aircraft up on a short local test flight.

They also enquired about the amount of fuel and type of bombs being loaded to give them an indication as to the target before the main briefing.

Even though the blokes out on the open dispersals were tired after working long hours, in all kind of weather, they still hung around until take-off time just in case their kite developed a fault. Only after their aircraft's navigation lights disappeared into the night sky would they slowly wander back to their billets in small groups chatting as they went about the days events and the job the aircrew were doing that night. Often they would be woken from a deep sleep by the sound of engines as the returning Lancs flew low overhead and then lay awake counting each one in. The first question posed to anyone returning to a billet from duty crew was, "which aircraft have not returned?" While every ground crew expected operational losses, they all hoped their aircraft would survive.

Briefings

Our CO on No. 61 Squadron seemed to regard Air Gunners as chaps who had just come along for the ride and seemed to think they used the briefing period for extra sleeping time. He developed the nasty habit of calling upon some unfortunate gunner to stand up and give a complete résumé of the briefing. In September 1944 before the raid on the Dortmund-Ems Canal he called upon a gunner to stand up and repeat all that had been said. This young Sergeant stood up and gave an excellent repeat of all our instructions and orders. The Wing Commander congratulated him but said 'Sergeant you have left out the most important thing, the object of the operation'.

The Sergeant replied 'Yes sir, the object is to breach the banks of the RIVER RHINE and drain it dry to make it useless to German barges'.

When the cheers had died down and order restored the Wing Commander said 'Gentlemen what you have just heard must NOT go beyond these four walls, because if Barnes Wallace hears about this he will make a bomb to do it and I for one do not wish to be around to take them'.

Aircraft Remembered

Many Squadron aircrew named a son or daughter after the aircraft that brought them safely through their tour of operations. Between 1st March and the end of May 1944, Pilot Officer Ted Stone and crew had flown 21 operations in Lancaster ED860 QR-N Nan. Before being rested from ops, the crew made an agreement that the first daughter born to the wife of a crew member would be called Nan after their aircraft.

As it turned out Ted's daughter was the first to be born at the end of 1944 and was promptly named Jennifer Nan Stone. Twenty-seven years later the famous wartime Lancaster was again remembered when his grand-daughter was christened Nanette.

P/O Donald Paul also named his son Roger after a Squadron aircraft code letter. This time it was Lancaster ME595 QR-R. Although Don flew in eleven other Squadron aircraft during his tour of operations. It was in QR-R that he flew most of his Battle of Berlin operations.

Skellingthorpe Memories by a WAAF called Joan

I remember the autumn early morning mist hanging over the runways like a shimmering veil as I picked mushrooms on the airfield before the rest of the camp was astir, and occasionally swimming in the cold water of the local quarry.

I remember, when ops were on, going down to the airfield with some of the other girls to wave the crews off as they left on their dangerous missions, and in the early hours listening for the faint sound of the first Lancaster home.

I remember hearing the terrifying sound of exploding ammunition when a plane crashed while making an emergency landing and the subdued grapevine gossip when one of our aircraft failed to return.

I remember the camp music circle run by Ken Hodges where we listened to old gramophone records with lights turned low and cycling alone across the airfield and feeling quite detached from what was happening all around.

I remember the last bus to camp from Lincoln was always overflowing with high spirited companions and the night we scrumped apples from the Group Captain's garden. Also the cold December day we liberated a Christmas tree for the WAAF's recreational institute.

I remember the warmth and kindness we received from the villagers of Skellingthorpe but most of all I remember my comrades in blue whose youthful optimism made bearable all the tragic events and hardships.

Crew of QR-Y April 1945. Back row: (l-r) W/O Walter McLean (N), F/S Gwyn Rees (E), Sgt Harold Heppenstall (BA), F/S Jimmy Huck (RG). Front Row: (l-r) Sgt Ted Beswick (MUG) F/S Ivor Soal (P), F/S Cecil Keys (W/OB)

F/O BC Fitch and crew L-R: A Lyons (B/A) Len Whitehead (MUG) Les Cromerty (RG) Bernard Fitch (P) Sid Jennings (N) Johnnie Taylor (F/E) C Kershaw (W/Op)

F/O Ray Lushey and crew Skellingthorpe 1944

P/O R A Dear's crew L-R: Jim Johnson (RG) Fred Charlton (F/E) Fred Reaves (N) Reg Dear (P) Front: Jack Anderson (W/Op) Charlie Aird (MUG)

Lancaster ND896 QR-Q Queenie July 1944 at RAF Skellingthorpe

Lancaster EE176 QR-M Mickey the Moocher was a Squadron Centenarian with 128 operational sorties

Lancaster DV232 QR-K dropped into the Trent after stalling on its final approach while returning from Mannheim 5th-6th September 1943

CHAPTER 19

OPERATIONAL DIARY OF LANCASTER ED860

Of the 6,500 Lancaster bombers that flew on operations with Bomber Command during the Second World War, only 34 survived long enough to be credited with more that 100 bombing sorties over enemy territory.

The first Lancaster to become a centenarian was ED860 QR-N Nan of No.61 Squadron at RAF Skellingthorpe on 27th June 1944. Followed seven days later by its great rival at RAF Skellingthorpe, ED588 VN-G George of No.50 Squadron. By the summer of 1944, Lancaster ED860 was looked upon by the Squadron aircrew as a lucky aircraft and a symbol of survival in the hostile skies over Germany.

The aircraft was manufactured by A.V.Roe at Woodford, Manchester in early 1943 and was assigned to No.156 Pathfinder Squadron based at RAF Warboys, Cambridgeshire, on 14th April 1943 and carried their Squadron aircraft code GT-N Nan.

After completing 25 Pathfinder operations during the Battle of the Ruhr and Hamburg with No.156 Squadron, ED860 was transferred to No.61 heavy bomber Squadron based at RAF Syerston on 20th August 1943 and flew its first operation as QR-N Nan to Berlin four days later. It would return another 19 times to the Big City over the following six months. No other Lancaster flew on every Berlin operation during the winter of 1943-44.

While with No.61 Squadron, Lancaster ED860 QR-N flew a total of 105 bombing operations in fourteen months before crashing on take-off for Bergen from RAF Skellingthorpe on 28th October 1944. It was struck off Squadron charge on 4th November 1944.

During its twenty months operational career, Lancaster ED860 had flown approximately 250,000 miles in 1,031 hours and completed 130 operations over enemy territory. It flew these operations during the most intense period of night fighter opposition during 1943-44 and has rightly been called QR-N Nan the Lancaster legend of No.61 Squadron.

LANCASTER Mk III ED860

Manufacturer	A.V.Roe - Woodford, Manchester.
Date	March 1943 - contract No. B692741
RAF Service	No.156 Sqdn. 14th April 1943 - 19th August 1943 No.61 Sqdn. 20th August 1943 - 4th November 1944
Operations	130 - **Flying hours** - 1031
Type	Four-engine heavy bomber.
Crew	Seven - Pilot, Flight Engineer, Navigator, Bomb Aimer, Wireless Operator, Mid-Upper Gunner, Tail-Gunner.
Engines	Packard Merlin 28. 4 x 1460 h.p.
Dimensions	Length - 69.6 feet. Height - 20.6 feet. Wing Span - 102 feet. Wing Area - 1,297 sq.feet.
Weight	Empty - 41,000 lbs. Fully Loaded - 68,000 lbs.
Pay Load	Bomb bay 33 feet 0 inch Maximum bomb load 14,000lb. Fuel capacity - 2,154 gallons Maximum combined bomb and fuel load 27,000 lb.
Armament	Eight 0.303 inch machine guns in three turrets - Nose and dorsal turrets - two 0.303 inch Brownings, tail turret four 0.303 inch Brownings.
Performance	Rate of climb - 480 feet per min. Ceiling - 24,500 feet. Max. speed - 287 m.p.h. at 11,500 feet. Cruising speed - 216 m.p.h. Range with max. bomb load - 1,500 miles. Range with max. fuel load - 3,150 miles.

Note: These statistics are the manufacturers typical figures for a Mk.III Lancaster in use during 1944. Maximum performance was rarely achieved with a maximum fuel and bomb load under operational conditions.

Type of Aircraft	Mark	R.A.F. Number
LANCASTER	III	ED 860.

Contractor	Contract No.	Engine installed :—
		Merlin 28.
		Maker's airframe No. :—
A. V. Roe	B69274/40	

Unit or Cat'y/Cause	Station or Contractor	Date	Authority	41 or 43 Gp. Allot.
156 Sqdn		14.4.43	1632/256	
61 Sqdn	—	20.8.43	117 23/8	
R.O.S.	Cat AC	30.8.44	FB/A329	
61 Sqdn	18.10.44		CRO	
28.10.44	[illegible] / FB	29/10	17.402	
	S.O.C.	14.11.44	Pg 45 7/11	

A.M. Form 78

Lancaster ED860 Record Card

TYPICAL LANCASTER BOMB LOADS 1942-1945

The bomb loads listed below are approximate and depended upon the bomb/fuel mix to the Lancasters maximum gross take-off weight of 68,000 lbs.

AREA BOMBING RAIDS
(Maximum blast and incendiary attack)
Executive code word **USUAL.** This was the most frequently used Lancaster bomb load. It consisted of one 4000 lb Amatol, Minol or Tritonal filled Cookie, impact fused HC bomb with 12 small bomb carriers (SBC) each loaded with either 24 x 30 lb or 236 x 4 lb No.15 or 15X incendiary bombs.

AREA BOMBING RAIDS
(Industrial demolition of factories, rail yards and dockyards)
Executive code word **ABNORMAL.** Nominally a 14,000 lb bomb load consisting of 14 x 1000 lb MC, GP, RDX or American short-finned HE bombs with a mix of instantaneous nose armed fuses and long delay tail armed fuses up to 144 hours.

AREA BOMBING RAIDS
(Demolition of heavily industrialised cities by blast and fire)
Executive code word **COOKIE/PLUMDUFF.** This bomb load consisted of one 4000 lb with impact fuse, 3 x 1000 lb short-finned, short delay, tail armed HE bombs, plus up to six SBCs loaded with 4 lb or 30 lb incendiaries.

AREA BOMBING RAIDS
(Blast and demolition of heavily industrialised areas)
Executive code word **PLUMDUFF-PLUS.** This bomb load consisted of one 8000 lb HC bomb filled with 5,361 lb of Amotex with a barometric or impact fuse, plus up to 6 x 500 lb MC or GP bomb fitted with either instantaneous or long-delay fuses.

AREA BOMBING RAIDS
(Maximum incendiary attack against high density building targets)
Executive code word **ARSON.** Nominally a 14,000 lb bomb load consisting of 14 x SBCs each loaded with 236 x 4 lb No.15 incendiary and No.15X explosive incendiary (1 in 10 mix).

CARPET BOMBING OF TACTICAL TARGETS - V weapon launch and storage installations, mobile armour, artillery and troop concentrations.
Executive code word **NO BALL.** Bomb load consisted of one 4000 lb HC with impact fuse and up to 18 x 500 lb MC or GP (short finned) with a mix of instantaneous and delay fuses.

DOCKS, FORTIFICATIONS, SHIPS
Executive code word **PIERCE.** Bomb load included up to six 2,000 lb armour piercing bombs with 0.05 sec. tail delay fuse. Plus 3 x 500 lb MC. SAP or GP or 3 x 250 lb GP

AIR-SEA MINE LAYING SORTIES (Mines were dropped in enemy coastal shipping lanes and river estuaries)
Executive code word **GARDENING.** The Admiralty requirement on such sorties was for each aircraft to drop up to six parachute mines with either magnetic or acoustic activators.

SPECIAL BOMB LOADS; requiring aircraft modifications

SUBMARINE PENS, V-WEAPON STORAGE AND ASSEMBLY AREAS.
Executive code word **TALLBOY.** This spin-stabilised 12,000 lb deep penetration bomb consisted of 5,760 lb of Torpex D, usually with a triple fuse with a 0.01 sec. delay. Carried by Lancasters with bulged bomb doors.

EXCEPTIONALLY STRONG STRUCTURES;
Executive code word **GRAND SLAM**. This spin-stabilised 22,400 lb deep penetration bomb contained 11,000 lb of Torpex D, carried by light-weight Lancaster without bomb doors.

OPERATIONAL DIARY OF LANCASTER ED860

The following Operational Diary of Lancaster ED860 gives some indication of the high demands placed upon No.156 and No.61 Squadron's aircrew and ground staff by Bomber Command during the bombing offensive against Germany in 1943-44.

RAF Warboys No.156 (Pathfinder) Squadron, No.8 Group.
Aircraft code GT-N Nan

BATTLE Of THE RUHR - 20th April - 23rd July 1943

	Target		Ops No	A/C Captain
April 1943				
20-21	Stettin	Docks/oil plant	1	P/O J.N.Horan
26-27	Duisburg	Inland port	2	P/O J.N.Horan
30-1	Essen	Krupps factory	3	F/Lt D.T.Muir
May 1943				
4-5	Dortmund	Steel factory/docks	4	F/O B.F.Smith
13-14	Pilsen	Skoda armaments factory	5	Sgt L.W.Overton
23-24	Dortmund	Steel factory/docks	6	F/S D.L.Wallace
25-26	Düsseldorf	Blitz/industrial	7	F/S D.L.Wallace
29-30	Wuppertal	Blitz	8	Sgt L.W.Overton
June 1943				
11-12	Münster	Rail installations	9	F/Lt R.E.Young
12-13	Bochum	Blitz/industrial	10	F/Lt R.E.Young
16-17	Cologne	(Aborted)	11	F/Lt R.E.Young
19-20	Montchanin	Power station	12	F/Lt R.E.Young
21-22	Krefeld	Blitz	13	F/Lt R.E.Young
24-25	Elberfeld	Blitz	14	F/Lt R.E.Young
28-29	Cologne	Blitz/industrial	15	Sgt C.W.Wilkins
July 1943				
3-4	Cologne	Blitz/industrial	16	F/Lt A.L.McGrath
8-9	Cologne	Blitz/industrial	17	F/Lt R.E.Young

BATTLE OF HAMBURG - 24th July - 3rd August 1943

	Target		Ops No	A/C Captain
July 1943				
24-25	Hamburg	Blitz/industrial	18	F/Lt R.E.Young
27-28	Hamburg	Blitz/industrial	19	F/Lt R.E.Young
29-30	Hamburg	Blitz/industrial	20	F/Lt R.E.Young
August 1943				
2-3	Hamburg	Blitz/industrial	21	F/Lt R.E.Young

ITALIAN INTERLUDE - 7th August - 16th August 1943

7-8	Turin	Blitz/industrial	22	W/O G.Denwood
9-10	Mannheim	Blitz/industrial	23	W/O G.Denwood
10-11	Nuremberg	Blitz/industrial	24	W/O G.Denwood
15-16	Milan	Railway/Alfa Romeo works	25	P/O P.A.Coldham

After No.8 Group Pathfinder squadrons had completed a series of H2S equipment trials during June-July 1943, No.156 Squadron re-equipped with Lancasters fitted with the latest improved version of the new blind bombing equipment.

Lancaster ED860 was transferred to No.61 Squadron RAF Syerston, 20th August 1943 and became QR-N

BATTLE of BERLIN (August 1943 - March 1944)
No.61 Squadron RAF Syerston

	Target		Ops No	A/C Captain
August 1943				
23-24	Berlin	Blitz/industrial	26	Sgt M.C.Lowe
27-28	Nuremberg	Blitz/industrial	27	F/S J.G.McAlpine
31-1	Berlin	Blitz/industrial	28	Sgt E.Wielsher
September 1943				
2-3	Texel	Sea mine laying	29	F/O B.C.Fitch
3-4	Berlin	Blitz/industrial	30	Sgt E.Wielsher
5-6	Mannhiem	Blitz/industrial	31	Sgt E.Wielsher
6-7	Munich	Blitz/industrial	32	P/O E.Wielsher
September 1943				
22-23	Hannover	Blitz/industrial	33	P/O E.Wielsher
23-24	Mannhiem	Blitz/industrial	34	P/O E.Wielsher
27-28	Hannover	Blitz/industrial	35	P/O J.G.McAlpine
29-30	Bochum	Blitz/industrial	36	P/O J.G.McAlpine
October 1943				
1-2	Hagen	U-boat spares factory	37	P/O H.N.Scott
3-4	Munich	Blitz/industrial	38	P/O H.N.Scott
4-5	Frankfurt	Blitz/industrial	39	P/O J.F.McLean
7-8	Stuttgart	Blitz/industrial	40	P/O J.G.McAlpine
8-9	Hannover	Blitz/industrial	41	F/O H.N.Scott
18-19	Hannover	Blitz/industrial	42	F/O H.N.Scott
20-21	Leipzig	Blitz/industrial	43	F/O B.C.Fitch
22-23	Kassel	Blitz	44	F/O H.N.Scott

November 1943				
3-4	Düsseldorf	Blitz/industrial	45	F/O B.C.Fitch
10-11	Modane	Railway yards/tunnel	46	F/O H.N.Scott
16 November No.61 Squadron moved to RAF Skellingthorpe				
18-19	Berlin	Blitz/industrial	47	F/O B.C.Fitch
22-23	Berlin	Blitz/industrial	48	F/O H.N.Scott
23-24	Berlin	Blitz/industrial	49	F/O H.N.Scott
26-27	Berlin	Blitz/industrial	50	F/O H.N.Scott
December 1943				
2-3	Berlin	Blitz/industrial	51	P/O D.Paul
16-17	Berlin	Blitz/industrial	52	F/O H.N.Scott
20-21	Frankfurt	Blitz	53	F/O B.C.Fitch
23-24	Berlin	Blitz/industrial	54	F/O H.N.Scott
29-30	Berlin	Blitz/industrial	55	F/Lt H.N.Scott
January 1944				
1-2	Berlin	Blitz/industrial	56	F/Lt H.N.Scott
2-3	Berlin	Blitz/industrial	57	F/O B.C.Fitch
5-6	Stettin	Port/oil installations	58	P/O V.McConnell

12th January No.61 Squadron moved to RAF Coningsby

	Target		**Ops No**	**A/C Captain**
January 1944				
14-15	Brunswick	Blitz/industrial	59	F/O B.C.Fitch
20	Berlin	Blitz/industrial	60	F/Lt H.N.Scott
21-22	Berlin	Blitz/industrial	61	F/Lt H.N.Scott
27-28	Berlin	Blitz/industrial	62	P/O E.A.Stone
28-29	Berlin	Blitz/industrial	63	F/Lt H.N.Scott
30	Berlin	Blitz/industrial	64	F/Lt H.N.Scott
February 1944				
15	Berlin	Blitz/industrial	65	F/Lt H.N.Scott
19-20	Leipzig	Blitz/industrial	66	F/Lt H.N.Scott
20-21	Stuttgart	Blitz/industrial	67	F/Lt H.N.Scott
24-25	Schweinfurt	Ball bearing factory	68	F/Lt H.N.Scott
25-26	Augsburg	Aircraft factory	69	F/Lt H.N.Scott
March 1944				
1-2	Stuttgart	Bosch/Benz factory	70	P/O E.A.Stone
10-11	Châteauroux	Aircraft factory	71	P/O E.A.Stone
15-16	Stuttgart	Blitz/industrial	72	P/O E.A.Stone
18-19	Frankfurt	Blitz/industrial	73	P/O E.A.Stone
22-23	Frankfurt	Blitz/industrial	74	P/O E.A.Stone
24-25	Berlin	Blitz/industrial	75	P/O E.A.Stone
30-31	Nuremberg	Blitz/industrial	76	P/O E.A.Stone

Summary of Lancaster ED860 QR-N's Battle of Berlin Targets

Berlin	20	Hannover	4
Stuttgart	4	Frankfurt	4
Nuremberg	2	Leipzig	2
Munich	2	Mannhiem	2
Schweinfurt	1	Modane	1
Stettin	1	Kassel	1
Hagen	1	Châteauroux	1
Brunswick	1	Düsseldorf	1
Augsburg	1	Bochum	1
Texel	1		

Total = 51 Operations.

PRE-INVASION TARGETS 1st April - 6th June 1944

	Target		Ops No	A/C Captain
April 1944				
5-6	Toulouse	Aircraft factory	77	P/O E.Williams
10-11	Tours	Rail yards	78	P/O E.A.Stone
11-12	Aachen	Blitz	79	P/O E.A.Stone
	15th April Squadron moved back to RAF Skellingthorpe			
18-19	Juvisy	Rail yards	80	P/O E.A.Stone
20-21	Paris	Rail junction	81	P/O E.A.Stone
22-23	Brunswick	Industrial	82	P/O E.A.Stone
24-25	Munich	Blitz	83	P/O E.A.Stone
26-27	Schweinfurt	Ball bearing factory	84	P/O E.A.Stone
28-29	St.Médard-en-Jalles	Explosives factory	85	P/O E.A.Stone
29-30	St.Médard-en-Jalles	Explosives factory	86	P/O E.A.Stone
May 1944				
3-4	Mailly-le-Camp	Military camp	87	P/O E.A.Stone
6-7	Louailles	Ammunition dump	88	P/O E.A.Stone
8-9	Brest	Docks/Sea plane base	89	P/O E.A.Stone
10-11	Lille	Rail yard	90	P/O D.Street
19-20	Tours	Rail yard	91	P/O E.A.Stone
21-22	Duisburg	Blitz	92	P/O E.A.Stone
22-23	Brunswick	Blitz	93	P/O R.J.Auckland

24-25	Eindhoven	Philips factory	94	P/O R.J.Auckland
May 1944				
27-28	Nantes	Rail junction/workshops	95	F/O B.S.Turner
31-1 June	Saumur	Rail junction	96	Sgt F.E.Hardy

Aircraft taken off operations for major servicing until 19th June 1944

Lancaster ED860 QR-N Nan completed her 100th operation 27-28 June 1944

F/O B.S.Turner's crew and ground staff with the new centenarian

F/O Norman Hoad and crew wait for the armourers to finish loading QR-N Nan for its 120th operation. The crew L-R: K.O.Ball (N) W.H.Pullin (B/A) C.V.Embury (RG) N.England (MUG) G.P.Boyd (W/Op) C.S.Webb (F/E)

NORMANDY - Communication / Transport / V1 Sites

	Target		Ops No	A/C Captain
June 1944				
19-20	Watten	Flying bomb store	97	F/O B.S.Turner
21-22	Limoges	Aero engine factory	98	F/O B.S.Turner
24-25	Prouville	Flying bomb store	99	F/O B.S.Turner
27-28	**Vitry**	**Rail yard**	**100**	**F/O B.S.Turner**
29	Beauvoir	Flying bomb store	101	F/O B.S.Turner
July 1944				
4-5	St.Leu d'Esserent	Flying bomb store	102	F/O B.S.Turner
14-15	Villeneuve	Rail yard	103	F/O B.S.Turner
15-16	Never	Rail yard	104	F/O B.S.Turner
18	Caen	Op Goodwood support	105	F/O B.S.Turner
18-19	Revigny	Rail yard	106	F/O D.G.Bates
20-21	Courtrai	Rail junction	107	F/S W.McPherson
24-25	Donges	Oil depot	108	F/O C.N.Hill
25	St.Cyr	Airfield/signal depot	109	F/S A.H.Harrison
26-27	Givors	Rail junction	110	F/S A.H.Harrison
28-29	Stuttgart	Blitz	111	F/S A.H.Harrison
30	Cahagnes	Army support	112	F/S A.H.Harrison
31	Rilly-la-Montage	Rail tunnel	113	F/Lt B.S.Turner
August 1944				
1	Siracourt	Flying bomb site	114	F/Lt B.S.Turner
2	Bois De Cassan	Flying bomb site	115	F/Lt B.S.Turner
5	St.Leu d'Esserent	Flying bomb store	116	F/Lt B.S.Turner
6	Bois De Cassan	Flying bomb site	117	F/O E.R.Church
7-8	Secqueville	Army support	118	F/O N.E.Hoad
9-10	Châtellerault	Oil storage	119	F/O N.E.Hoad
11	Bordeaux	U-boat pens	120	F/O N.E.Hoad
13-14	Rüsselsheim	Opel factory	121	F/O N.E.Hoad
August 1944				
14	Brest	U-boat pens/shipping	122	W/O D.R.Souter
15	Gilze-Rijen	Night fighter airfield	123	W/O D.R.Souter
16-17	Stettin	Port/industrial	124	F/O N.E.Hoad
18	Bordeaux	Oil storage depot	125	F/O J.S.Cooksey
August 1944				
19	La Pallice	Oil storage depot	126	F/O J.S.Cooksey
25-26	Darmstadt	Blitz	127	W/O D.R.Souter
26-27	Königsberg	Port/blitz	128	W/O D.R.Souter
27-28	Königsberg	Port/blitz	129	F/O N.E.Hoad

Aircraft main spar damaged by night fighter attack. Aircraft repaired at RAF Skellingthorpe by outside contractor.

October 1944

23	Flushing	Flak batteries	130	F/O L.A.Pearce
28	Bergen	U-boat pens	...	F/O L.A.Pearce

(Aircraft crashed on take-off 22.39 hours)

CRASH DETAILS

ED860 QR-N crew

Pilot	F/O L.A.Pearce
Flt.Eng.	Sgt J.B.Murray
Navigator	F/S R.B.Pettigrew
Bomb Aimer	Sgt D.A.Barker
Wireless Op.	F/S A.Perry
Air Gunner	Sgt A.Barker
Air Gunner	Sgt R.Gillanders

Take-off Time 22.39 hours Weather at Base: Moonlight but poor visibility

Since joining the R.A.A.F. in 1943. F/O Laurence Pearce, the crew's young Australian skipper, had logged a total of 211 flying hours on various type of aircraft. Although his experience in flying Lancaster heavy bombers at night was only 20 hours, he had been entrusted to further the 130 operational total of QR-N Nan with this sortie to Bergen.

At 22.35 hours F/O Pearce lined up the Lancaster at the end of the Skellingthorpe main runway and opened the throttles against the brakes to see if all four Merlin engines responded evenly. He then throttled back, released the brakes and began to re open the throttles again. The heavily loaded aircraft slowly built up speed until it was thundering down the runway, but before the young Aussie pilot had full rudder control a dangerous swing developed and the aircraft swung violently to port hitting a runway glim lamp which burst a tyre and the undercarriage collapsed. The resulting ground loop tore off part of the port wing spilling high octane fuel from ruptured tanks and by the time the aircraft finally came to a halt the heavy fuel and bomb load had crushed the bomb bay doors and lower fuselage. Before the emergency services arrived on the scene, all the crew had managed to scramble out of the aircraft and distance themselves from a very dangerous situation. They were all feeling very shaken after such a devastating experience, but otherwise unhurt.

Early next morning a 58MU crash party arrived in a convoy of trucks containing a Lorain crane, jacks, inflatable airbags, bogie wheels etc. They were met by the station Armament Officer who informed them he had cordoned off the area because the aircraft still had fuel and high explosive bombs on board. He then quickly withdrew from the scene.

After pumping the aircraft's fuel into a bowser, the crash crew used the crane to lift the bomber to a height which allowed them to place bogies under the wings. They then faced the problem of defusing the bomb load in QR-N's crushed bomb-bay. Fortunately, everything went well and by the end of the day the aircraft had been dismantled and taken away aboard four 60 feet long Queen Mary lorries.

Over the previous 18 months QR-N Nan had successfully carried out 130 operations and survived night fighter attacks and the heavy flak thrown up at her over the Ruhr valley and during the battle of Berlin.

Everyone connected with the aircraft at RAF Skellingthorpe was disappointed that such a distinguished aircraft should be destroyed in this way. In fact the Squadron CO was so angry, he ordered Flying Officer Pearce to visit all the ground trade section huts and apologise to the ground staff for this avoidable accident.

A.M. FORM 1180

+15 +16 +A +B DNGY. | JAN FEB MAR | APR MAY JUN | JUL AUG SEP | OCT NOV DEC | PERIOD | OTU | AFU (P) | AFU (O) | SFTS | EFTS | +18 | 2 ENG | 1 ENG | 1 | 2 | 3 | 4 | 5 | 6 | 7 | 8 | 9 | 10 | 11 | 12 | 13 | 14 | 15 | 16 | 17 | B | F | C | FT | +17

UNIT CLASS | AIRCRAFT TYPE | COMMAND

DATE	28 10 44
UNIT	61 SQN
OP. N.	op
GRP	5
COM	B
A.O.	AO
SIG.	AH02
F	B
A/C TYPE MARK	Lancaster 3
CODE	4-2
NO.	ED860
DAMAGE	B
COST	
765(C)	138
ENG. TYPE SINGLE/PORT/O	Merlin 28
Engine nos. / damage	266507 B.; 249453 B; 327086 B; 325028 B
1668	/
PORT/I	
STBD/I	
STBD/O	
412 / PR	
REP AIB. NO.	
FILE	G.81165/44
OTHER A/C UNIT	
OTHER TYPE	
CNTY.	Lincs.
A/P	Skellingthorpe
PLACE	
R.A.F. (People in aircraft, U)	7
TOT.	7

ENG. TROUBLE | ENGINE | M D G PM PP PH PC ALL. PET. ALL. E.

CAT.: E B AC A AR U FATAL INJ.

OUT A C: I K | PEOPLE IN AIRCRAFT: U 1(S) I K M TOT.

FUNCTION	NAME, INITIALS, NATIONALITY	RANK	NUMBER	TOTAL SOLO TOTAL	TOTAL SOLO TYPE	NIGHT SOLO TOTAL	NIGHT SOLO TYPE	INST LINK	CAS.
Pilot	PEARSE L.A. (Aus)	A/F/O	424820	211	29	78	20		N

XPF XAA XQQ XBB PARA. PROPS GUNS OXYGN BRK. UP — SPECIAL

O P / C P / S P / P F F A — PILOT

L T O F I M FS ILOC/IOC ILCG — STAGE

S.D. 96

+19 +1 +2 +3 +6 +5 +4 +12 +11 +10

51-7579. PAT. NOS. 225069. 297992. C.C. 96092 H

ACCIDENT REPORT

ILCG
ILOC/IOC
FS
M
I
F
O
T
L
C P
O P
BRK UP
OXYGN
GUNS
PROPS
PARA
XBB
XQQ
XAA
XFF
DNGY.
+16
5

STAGE · PILOT · SPECIAL

1 2 3 4 5 6 7 +9 FIRE COL.RES. OPS DUAL INS NIGHT U UCD U UD UB U UTWF A AF A AI A AR A AM OTHER X O X G X L X C W V W W W I +8 +7 +6 +5 +4 +3 +2 +1 +19 INJ. FATAL

ACC. CODE NO. | FLIGHT | UNDER CARRIAGE | AIRFRAME | EXTERNAL | WEATHER

FLIGHT — H — M DAY/NIGHT N DUAL/(SOLO)/2 PILOTS DUTY Bombing ops

ACC. 22·39 HRS. DAY/NIGHT N LIGHT MOON

O/C

A ok

P SS

Taking off a/c swung port while left runway & tyre burst on striking flip lamps, in violent swing u/c collapsed.

Inexp. in correcting initial swing. N.F.A.

E ok

U T B · USM

A. ok

X ok

W ok

type burst (after swing off runway) + u/c collapsed due to ~~[struck out]~~ resultant violent swing.

poor vis. + poor weather conditions generally.

SP. REC.

ADDITIONAL EVIDENCE — A.I.B. INVEST C. of I. OTHER — AOC LBE Disobedience of Orders.

FIRE

BLAME AND DISCIP. ACTION LBE (Rea)

CAT. U AR A AC B E

ENGINE ALL E ALL PET PC PH PP PM G D M

UR

ACCIDENT REPORT

After the crash QR-N's wireless operator Bill Perry wrote the following in his war diary

> **Saturday 28th Oct. 1944**
> **"Ops on Bergen in N for Nan (night). Did not take-off as plane swung on take-off and crashed at 65 miles per hour with full bomb load on board. Undercart collapsed and starboard outer torn off. Bomb bay wrecked and nose smashed in.**
> **We were very lucky as bombs did not go off, Jock the engineer suffered the only injuries (a cut face sustained when falling off cockpit when abandoning plane). The end of Nan, a complete write off. SHE WAS A LUCKY KITE RIGHT TO THE END".**

Lancaster MkIII ED860 QR-N Nan was declared Cat.E, (Aircraft is a write off). The aircraft was struck off charge (S.O.C.) on 4th November 1944.

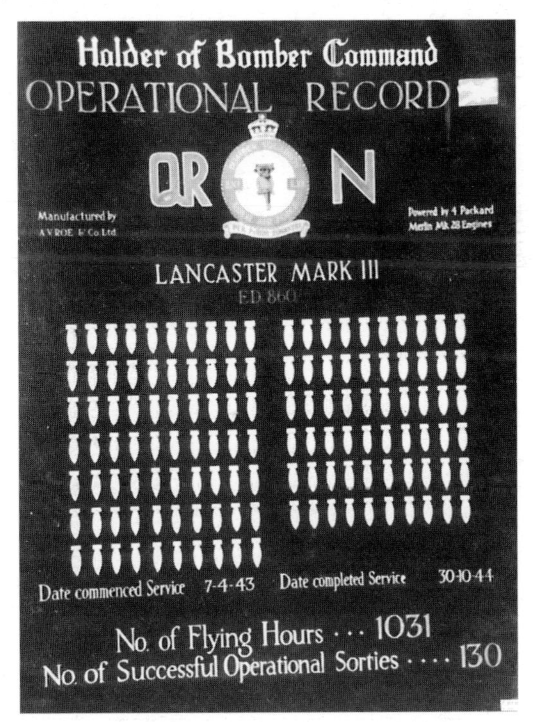

Lancaster ED860 QR-N Nan mounted bomb panel

Lancaster MkIII ED860 Operational Record

- Bomber Command Service 14th April 1943-28 October 1944
- No.156 (Pathfinder) Squadron 14th April-19th August 1943
- Total Pathfinder Operation Sorties = 25
- No.61 Squadron (5 Group) 20th August 1943 - 4th November 1944
- Total Heavy Bomber Operational Sorties = 105
- Flew the highest number of Lancaster Berlin sorties (20).
- First Lancaster to reach 100 sorties over enemy territory, 27th June 1944.
- Total Operational Sorties = 130
- Total Flying Hours = 1,031

Skellingthorpe's centenarians QR-N Nan and VN-G George August 1944

This poem was written by a member of No.61 Squadron while at RAF Skellingthorpe in 1944 and given to his girlfriend. She was one of the local girls who befriended the airmen at the Parklands pub in Lincoln.

THE LANCASTER

Her name was Nan she was one of the best
But that was the night I gave her the test
I looked at her with such joy and delight
For she was mine for just one night

She looked so pretty, so neat and so slim
The night was dark, the lights so dim
I was so excited my heart missed a beat
Because I just knew I was in for a treat

I've seen her stripped, I've seen her bare
I felt all around her and looked everywhere
I got her up high as quick as I could
I handled her well, for she was so good

There is no doubt, she's the best in the land
This four-engine Lancaster of Bomber Command

By one of the Brylcream boys

CHAPTER 20

THE BEGINNING OF THE END

By the spring of 1944 No.61 Squadron was again operating from RAF Skellingthorpe, and from the start of April supported the Second Front preparations by attacking transport, communications, submarine pens and oil depot targets in France.

After the D-Day landings in Normandy on 6th June 1944, the Squadron supported the Allied ground forces with daylight raids against enemy troop concentrations, V1 rocket launching sites and storage locations in France before returning once again to hostile skies over Germany in August 1944.

At the end of August the Squadron flew two extreme range operations to the Baltic port of Königsburg which was an important supply port for the German army fighting on the eastern front. Although the target was some 950 miles away from the bomber bases the second raid on 29th-30th August, turned out to be one of the most successful 5 Group operations of the war. This was mainly due to the determination and courage of the 189 Lancaster crews and the skill of the Master Bomber, Wing Commander J Woodroffe, who delayed the main force attack until the Pathfinders marked the target through a break in the clouds.

Unfortunately due to the delay, the attacking force met heavy night fighter opposition over the target area which resulted in the loss of fifteen aircraft (7.9%). Amongst the aircraft taking part from RAF Skellingthorpe were two veteran Lancasters, ED588 VN-G George of No.50 Squadron on its 128th operation and ED860 QR-N Nan of No.61 Squadron on its 129th operation. Both aircraft came under fighter attack during the raid. These attacks resulted in VN-G George crashing in Sweden and QR-N Nan returned to Skellingthorpe with damage from a 20mm cannon shell which exploded between the wing root and starboard inner fuel tank.

The Squadron continued to fly operations from Skellingthorpe throughout the winter of 1944-45 against German industrial targets and also in support of the Allied armies advance towards Germany. During this period the names of Brunswick, Nuremburg, Walcheren, Darmstadt, Düsseldorf, Dortmund-Ems-Canal and Munich appeared in aircrew operation logbooks. In fact the Squadron participated in all the major bombing operations which No.5 Group squadrons flew during this final phase of the war. Amongst these operations was the outstandingly successful attack on the small town of Wesel situated on the north bank of the river Rhine. This raid took place on 23rd March 1945 and prepared the way for the Rhine crossings the following day by the Allied armies.

The last Squadron aircraft to be lost on operations during the five year conflict occurred on the 9th April 1945. When Lancaster RF121 QR-J failed to return from a daylight raid on Hamburg docks.

Ted Beswick in the mid-upper turret of QR-Y

Sgt Ted Beswick was the mid-upper gunner in Lancaster QR-Y and describes what happened.

This was a 5 Group daylight raid and No.50 and 61 squadron crews were briefed to attack the oil storage depot in the dock area of Hamburg. Also to fly within the bomber stream of 57 Lancasters was to attack the U boat pens with 14,00lb Tallboy and 22,000lb Grand Slam bombs.

My skipper was W/O Ivor Soar and after checking everything was ok with Lancaster QR-Y, took off from Skellinghorpe at 14:28 hrs. After Navigator W/O Walter McLean gave him a Westerly course to fly we all settled down in our crew positions while the heavily loaded aircraft gradually climbed up to our operational height of 16,800 ft. One hour after take off while flying over the Irish Sea, east of Belfast, we formed up with No.50, 61 and 617 squadron aircraft and then set course for Hamburg.

QR-Y was in the leading gaggle of aircraft as we ran up to the target area and I could see from my mid upper turret the black puffs of smoke from the predicted flak box barrages. The flak gradually reached the bomber stream and soon we were all flying through a sky that seemed to be full of exploding shells.

The Squadron started the attack at 17.30 hrs and while on our bombing run the aircraft was hit by shrapnel in the nose and our bomb aimer, Sgt Harold Heppenstall, was slightly wounded in his left arm. He was able to carry out his duties and dropped our bomb load at the aiming point.

We had just left the target area when the Lancaster behind us, QR-J piloted by F/Lt Paul Greenfield DFC, suddenly reared up violently and exploded in a ball of fire.

Seconds later a German twin engine Me 262 jet fighter appeared flying past the pall of smoke and flaming wreckage of QR-J.

Our rear gunner, F/S Jimmy Huck, opened fire immediately but I couldn't get my guns down low enough so I yelled out to the skipper 'corkscrew port go' but due to the close proximity of other aircraft he responded with a shallow dive.

On leveling out, the Me 262 was about 75 yards off our port beam and turning to line up on another Lanc some 200 yards ahead. I opened fire with my twin 0.303 Brownings and saw a number of strikes along the fuselage followed by black smoke from the cockpit area. The fighter then rolled over and dived out of sight.

Taffy Rees, our flight engineer yelled out over the I/C 'we've got him' and this was confirmed by the skipper and rear gunner.

It's funny how time slows down in combat situations. From start to finish the whole incident happened in less than 30 seconds.

Crew members who died in Lancaster RF121 QR-J were: F/Lt A P Greenfield DFC, P/O W J A Gibb, F/S W J Haddon, F/S J R King and W/O V P Smith

The only crew members to survive the jet fighter's attack were the flight engineer and rear gunner.

The Me 262 fighter pilot was JG/7 Staffelkapitan Hauptmann Franz Schall. He was the second highest scoring Me 262 ace of the war with 16 Kills. German records show that Hptm Schall died the following day in a flying accident.

Hamburg docks under attack by No.61 Squadron Lancasters

On 25th-26th April 1945 No.5 Group mounted Bomber Command's last heavy bomber operation of the war against the oil refinery at Tonsberg in southern Norway.

Twelve Mosquito pathfinders accurately placed their TIs over the target and the following main force of 107 Lancaster severely damaged the refinery with HE bombs.

For this raid, fourteen of the Squadron's aircraft took off from RAF Skellingthorpe shortly after 20.00 hours and soon joined up with the other main force Lancs as they headed northeast over the North Sea. However, four of the Squadron aircraft developed technical problems and the crews aborted the operation and jettisoned their bombs into the sea before returning to Skellingthorpe.

The Squadron's last mission during the Second World War was to assist other squadrons in Operation Exodus that was implemented just before the end of hostilities to bring home 75,000 ex-prisoners of war as quickly as possible. To this end the Squadron Lancasters ferried some 1,080 POWs to England from liberated air bases on the continent during the first two weeks of May 1945 without mishap.

VE Day 8th May 1945

There was no stand down at RAF Skellingthorpe on VE day as seven Squadron Lancasters took-off for airfields in Germany to continue with the Exodus operation. Those crews who were flying listened to the momentous announcements of the German defeat over their aircraft's radio while en-route for the continent.

In the evening VE celebrations were soon in full swing with an All Ranks station dance held in one of the airfield hangars.

VE+1 saw the Squadron's Wing Commander, C.W.Scott AFC, act as pilot to Air Vice Marshal H.A.Constantine AFC on the inaugural Cooks Tour of damaged German cities.

Flying continued throughout May with Operation Exodus, training flights and clearing the airfield of unserviceable bombs by dropping them into the North Sea. All this activity added up to 585 hours of non-operational flying by the Squadron's Lancasters during the month.

After five years of war and an uncertain future it was a time of very mixed emotions for everyone associated with the Squadron. F/Lt R.H.Hamer summarised the historic events of May 1945, and his personal feelings, in No.61 Squadron Operations Record Book as follows

May was a month of joys and disappointment. The first being the news of victory in Europe and the second, the breaking up of the old Squadron.

Jubilant Skellingthorpe aircrew May 1945

V.E. Parade through the City of Lincoln 4th June 1945

RAF Skellingthorpe WAAF contingent march along the crowd lined street.

CHAPTER 21

THE RECKONING

As one of the original members of No.5 Group Bomber Command, No.61 Squadron made a tremendous contribution to this premier Group's efforts in bringing about the final victory over Nazi Germany.

By the end of the war in Europe in May 1945, the Squadron had completed the second highest number of bombing raids overall in Bomber Command. They also flew the most raids by a Lancaster squadron between 1942-45.

As No.61 Squadron was always at the forefront of Bomber Command's bombing campaign against Germany, it is not surprising that they achieved one of the best heavy bomber squadron operational records during the conflict.

The following analysis shows a Royal Air Force service record of which everyone who served in The Lincoln Imp Squadron during World War Two can be justly proud.

OPERATIONAL PERFORMANCE: 1939-1945

Total

1939-1941	**Hampden:** 229 bombing + 49 mine laying + 2 leaflet	= 280
1941-1942	**Manchester:** 33 bombing + 11 mine laying	= 44
1942-1945	**Lancaster:** 351 bombing + 25 mine laying + 1 leaflet	= 377

Total Raids: 613 bombing + 85 mine laying + 3 leaflet = 701

		Operation Sorties	Aircraft Losses
1939-1941	**Hampden:**	1,339 sorties	28 aircraft lost (2.1%)
1941-1942	**Manchester:**	197 sorties	12 aircraft lost (6.1%)
1942-1945	**Lancaster:**	4,546 sorties	116 aircraft lost (2.6%)
	Totals:	**6,082 sorties**	**156 (2.6%) Losses**

In addition 25 Lancasters were destroyed in crashes in the U.K.

HIGHLIGHTED POINTS OF INTEREST

World War Two 1939-45:

- An operational squadron at the outbreak of war in September 1939.
- First squadron to bomb a land target in Germany - Hornum seaplane base, 19th March 1940.
- Took part in first Berlin raid on 25th-26th August 1940
- Participated in the epic low level daylight attack on Le Creusot 17th October 1942
- First squadron to use Lancaster Mk.II aircraft operationally
- Five squadron Lancasters flew on the first North African shuttle raid, 20th-23rd June 1943
- Took part in the attack on Peenemünde the V2 development site 17th-18th August 1943
- Flight Lieutenant W.Reid awarded Victoria Cross, Düsseldorf raid 3rd-4th November 1943.
- Flew on all 20 Berlin raids 23rd-24th August 1943 - 24th-25th March 1944
- Carried out more raids using the A.V. Roe Lancaster heavy bomber than any other squadron in Bomber Command.
- Achieved the second highest total of bombing raids in Bomber Command's heavy squadrons.
- Lancaster ED860 QR-N Nan became the first aircraft in Bomber Command to complete 100 sorties over enemy territory, 27th June 1944. It was also the only Lancaster in Bomber Command to fly on all 20 Berlin raids between 24th August 1943 - March 1944
- Four of No.61 Squadron Lancasters became veterans by surviving more than 100 bombing operations over enemy territory.
  These aircraft were: LL843 QR-P Pod 118, JB138 QR-J Just Jane 123, EE176 QR-M Mickey the Moocher 128 and ED860 QR-N Nan 130.
- Last Operation 25th-26th April 1945, Oil refinery at Tonsberg in southern Norway.
- Last Mission, Operation Exodus, Squadron Lancasters ferried 1,080 ex-PoWs home to England from the Continent.

CHAPTER 22

No.61 SQUADRON'S BOMBER COMMAND SERVICE: 1945-1958

After World War Two ended in May 1945, the Squadron remained part of the slimmed down post war Bomber Command. In May 1946 while at RAF Waddington the Squadron re-equipped with the new four-engine Avro Lincoln.

The Squadron became operational again in December 1950 after being sent on a three month detachment to Singapore (Tengah). From there the Squadron aircrews flew sorties as part of the Operation Firedog force against the communist terrorists in Malaya. In March 1954 the Squadron was called on again to another troubled spot in the crumbling British Empire. This time the Lincolns flew to Nairobi in Kenya to operate against the Mau Mau terrorists. Upon its return from Kenya in June 1954, the Squadron re-equipped with the English Electric Canberra B2 twin-engine jet medium bomber. Once fully equipped, the Squadron became part of the Wittering Wing and later the Upwood Wing.

With the latter it went to Nicosia (Cyprus) in October 1956 and flew operations against the Egyptians during the Suez canal campaign.

In January 1957 No.61 Squadron returned to RAF Upwood and remained in Bomber Command for another year before being disbanded at the end of March 1958.

RAF United Kingdom Airfields and Overseas Detachments:

STURGATE....................................June 1945-January 1946
WADDINGTON............................January 1946-August 1953
Detachments:
Hemswell ....July 1947-December 1947
Singapore ....December 1950-April 1951

Egypt (various times)........................1949-1953
Aden (various times)........................1949-1953
WITTERING..................................August 1953-June 1955
Detachment:
Kenya ....March 1954-June 1954
UPWOOD ....June 1955-March 1958
Detachment:
Cyprus...October 1956 - January 1957

No.61 SQUADRON DISBANDED AT RAF UPWOOD
31st MARCH 1958

AFTER 21 YEARS CONTINUOUS SERVICE IN BOMBER COMMAND

IN REMEMBRANCE

Sadly the victory over tyranny could not be achieved without loss of life.

Bomber Command sustained a total of 55,563 fatalities while training or on flying operations against Germany during the Second World War. Of these No.50 Squadron suffered 1,002 casualties and No.61 Squadron 981.

Two memorials are dedicated in remembrance of the young men and women who lost their lives while serving with these two bomber squadrons. One was erected by the No.50 & No.61 Squadrons Association and stands close to the site of the long gone main runway of RAF Skellingthorpe. The other, set in a memorial garden by the people of Skellingthorpe village has this poignant epitaph engraved upon it.

My brief sweet life is over
My eyes no longer see
No Christmas trees
No summer walks
No pretty girls for me
I've got the chop - I've had it
My nightly ops are done
Yet in another hundred years
I'll still be twenty-one

By: Sgt Ralph Wilson Gilbert
(Air gunner No.158 Sqdn 1944)

Nos.50 and 61 Squadrons Memorial in Birchwood Avenue, Lincoln

RAF Skellingthorpe Airfield and Control Tower circa 1963
The whole airfield has now disappeared under the Birchwood Housing Estate

ACKNOWLEDGEMENTS

I would like to thank the following people and organisations for their generous help in connection with the preparation of this book. Without their personal wartime stories and photographs this story could not have been told.

Ex-Members of No.61 Squadron
Cpl E.Ainley, Sgt E.T. Beswick, Sgt J.W.Boynton (No.156 Sqdn), P/O C.A.Cawthorne DFM, Sgt J.C.Chapman (No.156 Sqdn), P/O A.Clark DFC, F/O M.Chivers DFC, Sgt E.A.Davidson DFM, P/O R.A.Dear DFC, F/O J.H.Dyer, S/L I.G.Fadden, F/O B.C.Fitch DFC, Sgt C.J.Gray DFM, F/O N.E.Hoad, Sgt R Hoskisson, Sgt J.Johnson, LAC R.P.Meredith No.58 MU, P/O D.Paul, LAC R.Packer, F/Sgt D.G.Patfield, F/Lt W.Reid VC, Mrs R.D.Sherwin, Sgt L.Walker, LAC D.Watson, F/O J.Wheeler and Dutch historian Ad van Zantvoort.

The ranks and decorations shown above are those held by the above and quoted within this book and do not reflect the Royal Air Force rank or decoration attained at a later date by any individual.

I would also like to record a special thank you to my wife, Marjorie, for her loyal support, encouragement and the tremendous task she undertook to sort out my word processor shortcomings.

Institutions and Associations
The Public Record Office at Kew, The Imperial War Museum, The Royal Air Force Museum at Hendon, Bomber Command Association, Nos.50 & 61 Squadrons Association, No.156 Squadron Association, Cambridgeshire Records Office, Cambridgeshire Library Service, The Lincoln Local Studies Library and The Lincolnshire Echo.